Published by National Lampoon Press

National Lampoon, Inc. • 8228 Sunset Boulevard • Los Angeles • California • 90046 • USA
American Stock Exchange: NLN

NATIONAL LAMPOON, NATIONAL LAMPOON PRESS and colophon are trademarks of National Lampoon

Animal house / by Chris Miller -- 1st ed.

p. cm.

ISBN-10: 0-9788323-4-5

ISBN-13: 978-09788323-4-6

Book Design and Production by
JK NAUGHTON

Cover by
MoDMaN

Cover art by
Rick Meyerowitz

WWW.NATIONALLAMPOON.COM

The National Lampoon's
Animal House
Book

Written and Edited by

Chris Miller

From the screenplay by
Harold Ramis, Douglas Kenney & Chris Miller
and the Universal film directed by John Landis
and produced by Matty Simmons and Ivan Reitman

To my animal houses

Alpha Delta Phi – Dartmouth
1960-1964

Delta Tau Chi – Faber
1977

Chris Miller co-wrote the script to *National Lampoon's Animal House* with Harold Ramis and Doug Kenney starting with a treatment in December of 1975. The screenplay was then written during 1976 and 1977. He also wrote the short stories which inspired the film, "The Night of the Seven Fires" and "Pinto's First Lay," which appeared in *National Lampoon* in 1974 and 1975. Chris was also present for the entire *Animal House* shoot, and portrayed Delta brother Hardbar. Herewith are some of Chris' memories of the production, filmed in its entirety in Eugene and Cottage Grove, Oregon, in October and November 1977.

MY LIFE WITH THE ANIMALS – AGAIN
by Chris Miller

What I hadn't anticipated was how real it would feel. The fraternity basement, Otis Day and the Knights, the cute girls in togas, all of it. And that was definitely real beer in those cups, folks. Lots of the Deltas dancing to "Shout" did not have to *act* drunk. Me, for one. Figured I'd feel less ridiculous doing these old steps if I knocked back a few. I recall the toga party taking a week to shoot. By the second day, reality and fiction were running together. I almost felt I was back at the Alpha Delta Phi house at Dartmouth, and it was 1961 all over again.

Except that every so often our director, John Landis, would shriek *"Cut,"* and all of us wildly twisting and gatoring Deltas and our dates would come to a full stop, the music cutting off suddenly, and there we were, back in the real world. Just a movie set, after all. Then, once the camera guys had accomplished the next set-up, the music would roar back on and we'd all start dancing again. This meant that you would serially get drenched in sweat and then stand around shivering in the dank, chilly Oregon air, doing nothing for extended periods. The rear door to the basement (we were in a real University of Oregon fraternity basement) had to be left halfway open in order to allow electric cables to snake inside. This caused a constant draft, bringing to our nasal facilities the distinctive reek of the local paper mill. Lots of the actors and crew guys caught colds. Landis got so sick he had to sit in his director's chair sipping peppermint tea for several days, his voice practically gone, forbidden to say anything beyond "roll camera" and "cut." Still, the toga party was great fun and I wouldn't have missed it.

Landis had done a smart thing, I felt. He'd decided it would be great to have writers around should it become necessary to alter scenes or write new ones, and so had invited Doug Kenney and me to join the cast. In the script, there had been a Delta named Mountain, a big, friendly guy with a small part, but they never found an actor to play him. So Landis divided Mountain's moments between us. Doug became Stork and I suggested they call me Hardbar, after an actual fraternity brother who was famous for beating off more often than your average chimpanzee. Doug cannily made much of his role, donning glasses and one of those breast-pocket penholder-things, becoming the perfect ultrageek. He decided Stork was a math whiz and created a holster at his hip for his slide rule. (This was an item once used to multiply and do square roots and the like, before there were calculators. You know, back when people smoked pipes and used typewriters.) He would stand facing himself in the mirror, hand poised above the hook he'd taped to the rule, and I'd yell "Draw!" Doug got so he could whip the thing out and begin calculating in under two

Doug "Stork" Kenney and Chris "Hardbar" Miller

seconds. To his sorrow, he never got to display his quick-draw in the movie, as there was never a need for a Delta to calculate anything. But he made his character so unforgettable that Landis let him lead the band down that blind alley. As for me, I just followed John's directions. I gave Flounder a curious look when he asked "Are you guys playing cards?" I twisted in my toga, yelling "A little bit louder now" with Otis Day. When the man at the parade asked me to move so his little kid could see, I said "No!" It was my only line in the clear and since my voice wasn't picked up very well by the microphone, Landis later had to loop it in the studio. So that's actually John Landis' voice saying "No," not mine. But I did improvise and yell out "You tell 'em, Otter!" at the trial.

Meanwhile, when it turned out Donald Sutherland could give us a few days of his acting services, Doug came up with that classroom scene where Professor Jennings admits he finds Milton boring, too. We wrote some other scenes as well. So Landis got what he needed

and Doug and I got to watch this bizarre engine known as a movie production roll ever forward.

It has been said that movie shoots have much in common with military campaigns. The director is the general and everyone else is the army, and they're all supposed to function together to achieve difficult but desirable goals as quickly as possible. No days off! You can't fuck up! It's relentless. Landis – who the crew dubbed Outlandish – was the wackiest general to come along since Groucho in *Duck Soup*. The set was a happy, playful place because of John's exuberance. He was always surprising the actors with something or other. When the scene was shot with the brothers and new pledges singing "Louie Louie" around the jukebox, Landis stationed me and Doug on the stairs just behind them. He armed each of us with a pitcher of beer and told us we should, at his signal, dump the beer over the heads of the singers, who had no notion such a thing might happen to them. So – he signalled and we poured. The footage did not wind up in the movie, but I definitely enjoyed dumping a gallon of beer over the head of John Belushi.

People always ask about John. They seem to want some Belushi horror story. You know, he snorted a whole can of Drain-O the night before the parade sequence or something. Well, sorry, but my experience of John Belushi during the *Animal House* shoot was of a complete professional working at the peak of his powers. He was always on time and always knew his lines. He was focussed, cooperative, and crafted a brilliant Bluto – the other actors were in awe. *And* he was commuting each week between New York and Oregon, so he could continue his work with *Saturday Night Live* as well. I had total respect for this protean feat; it took a strong, strong man to handle all that he was handling, and all at the same time. There were no Belushi horror stories. He was a genial presence, as was his wife, Judy.

John was the only actor to get his own house. He was becoming quite the star. Back in New York, several of us associated with the *Lampoon* lived within a few blocks of each other in the Village—me, Doug, P. J. O'Roarke, Gerry Sussman, Rick Meyerowitz, and the Belushis. Before the shoot began I met John one Saturday morning on Bleeker Street to have breakfast at Al

& Ann's Luncheonette. So many people came up to talk to him that it took us an hour to walk the one block to the restaurant.

Everyone else in the movie company was quartered at a large motel complex outside Eugene called The Roadway Inn. There must have been three hundred rooms at that place. The actors were all in the same area. At night, different groups of us would coalesce, smoke weed, and sing and fool around until the middle of the night. Karen Allen played great guitar and gave good folk song. Each night a couple of us would steal the motel's piano and roll it to Bruce McGill's room, on the first floor by the stairs, and the music would go nonstop. Each morning the motel guys would come and roll the piano back again.

There was no big drug scene at during the shoot beyond weed, which was ubiquitous. After a while, the local dealers became aware of our presence and began showing up with exotic varieties of locally-grown shit. There may have been coke around, but the only time I saw any was after a meal one night, the first week we were there, around a long table in the Roadway Inn dining room. There must have been twelve of us; it was late and we had the place pretty much to ourselves. We'd drunk a bunch of wine and were in good spirits. After the waiter cleared the table and went off to find our desserts, one of those little bottles with a spoon attached came out of someone's pocket and made a single circuit of the table, each of us consuming a nice one-and-one. The conversation quickly became brighter and louder. This post-prandial toot seemed clearly superior to brandy, all agreed.

The album of the shoot was *Aja* by Steely Dan. Everyone seemed to have it. You walked down the hallways of the Inn and heard it coming from multiple rooms.

One day Ken Kesey and fellow Merry Prankster, Ken Babbs, showed up as we were shooting a scene in an outdoor location. They lived in the Eugene area, we were told. I came alive. My crazy pals and I, back in New York, had devoured Tom Wolfe's *The Electric Kool-Aid Acid Test* and thought the Pranksters were totally cool. A little group of actors and crew (and writers) stood

around as Babbs pulled out a couple of Js, lit up and passed them around. We felt that with this gesture the Kesey people were stamping our work with their imprimatur of hipness.

It felt that way when Sutherland showed up, too. The cast was mostly young, just getting their starts, and they had stars in their eyes at the sight of this veteran actor. Sutherland had been in the much-admired (though not by me) *M*A*S*H,* and his credentials both as a hipster and a movie star were impeccable. The inclusion of his deft, countercultural touch in the film once again felt like a certification of our coolness by the previous hip generation.

A very young Kevin Bacon was cast to play an obnoxious Omega pledge named Chip Diller. It was his first movie. In those days, Kevin's nose was more pushed up than it is now, making his nostrils flare dramatically. Each time he'd approach, Doug Kenney would cry *"Ewwwww!* You can see his *brains!"*

When the scene in which Otter picks up the dead girl's roommate was shot, the crew kept cracking up. Take after take, they'd explode with laughter. "Dead? Why, that minx! Did she put you up to this?" The camera guy, the gaffer, and the electrician roar anew. "Take 26," Landis

says tiredly. Otter smiles, all charm. "And could you get three dates for my friends?" "HAR HAR HAR HAR HAR!" goes the crew.

The actors were great fun to know. Bruce McGill was a fount of energy and laughter, a gas to hang out with. Karen Allen was a sweet, refreshing presence; there was many a crush on her, through cast and crew. John Vernon would plant himself at a table in the Roadway Inn bar nightly and down a long procession of drinks, gradually becoming incoherent. Boon and Otter, uh, I mean Peter Riegert and Tim Matheson, became like real fraternity brothers to me. Indeed, I began to think of all these movie people – not just the Deltas but everyone, really – as one big, coed fraternity, as dedicated as my old college frat was to forcing life to be fun. There's some very intense bonding on location shoots. Later, people go on to other movies or back to their lives and the thing fades, but then returns to life each time the cast, writers, producers and director are called together for some occasion, such as the 25th Animal House Anniversary in 2004, when Universal re-created the Faber College Homecoming Parade on Hollywood Boulevard. We love seeing each other. In case you were wondering, everyone feels a little awed at having been a part of the famous, iconic movie.

We knew Universal was starting to pay attention to what the crazies up in Oregon were doing when one day they sent us a crane. Landis, thrilled, started doing overhead shots left and right. The crane was another stamp of our authenticity; it meant the dailies we sent back to the studio were making the execs laugh. The further we went into the production, the happier Universal became, and so the happier *we* became. I think all that fun and enthusiasm on the set is right there on the screen when you watch the movie. What must it be like to be in the cast of a prison movie, or a smallpox epidemic movie, or a torture-chamber movie? *Animal House,* it occurs to me, is the absolute opposite of such films. It's about many things, but most importantly it's about *freedom,* man, and this may be a clue to its unending popularity. Who doesn't love freedom?

When Thanksgiving rolled around, there were only a few days of shooting left. Most of the leaves had fallen from the trees and, looking up, one beheld a Jackson Pollock of bare branches against a steely-gray sky. Universal threw a turkey dinner for one and all at the Roadway Inn dining room. D-Day, uh, Bruce had rolled the piano back himself this morning. It had sustained multiple body dings during its many transits but still sounded pretty good as people took turns playing it. When Cesare Danova, who portrayed the mobbed-up mayor of Faber, Carmine DePasto, strolled in with his wife, whoever was playing shifted abruptly to the "Theme from *The Godfather,"* and the entire room sang along. *Da-da-da-da-da-da-da-daaaah.* Cesare smiled broadly and made Pope-like gestures with his hands.

And then it was over. The production had utterly consumed all of us who worked on it. We'd grown used to its rhythms, and to having the shooting schedule structure our lives. Suddenly it was gone. Shit, now Doug and I would have to go back to New York, just as it became an arctic wasteland for the next three months, and start working for a living once again. I was supposed to write and edit the book version of the movie. I don't know what Doug was supposed to do. He was practically despondent. He'd been there from the start and now stood stubbornly in the freezing parking lot as the last of the generator trucks and honey wagons pulled out, never to return to the Roadway Inn. Was that a tear dangling from Dougie's eye? I seconded his emotion. But life went on. Later, though we were both involved with many other movies, none of them gave us the happy rush that working on *Animal House* had. To paraphrase Flounder, "Oh, boy, was it *great!"*

List of Chapters

1 Rush Week 1

2 Sink Night 15

3 School Begins 25

4 Pinto's First High 35

5 There Were Giants in Those Days 41

6 Bluto's Midnight Peep 47

7 Midterms 59

8 Toga Party 65

9 Trial 79

10 Road Trip 85

11 Black Friday 93

12 There Are Giants in These Days 103

Fraternity Row
Faber College 1962

WELCOME TO FABER COLLEGE
FRESHMAN ORIENTATION PAMPHLET
FALL, 1962

EMIL FABER
FOUNDER A.D. 1904

KNOWLEDGE IS GOOD

A MESSAGE FROM THE DEAN...

Vernon Wormer, Dean of Students

Each September, new freshmen arrive lugging suitcases bursting with questions and clean socks. "Where's Dorkner Lunatarium?" they ask clued-in sophomores.

"Can co-eds matriculate standing up?"

"What are nonrefundable meal tickets and the Truth?"

"Is this O.K.?"

And many more. To answer these questions, I'd like to tell you the true story of two Faber College freshmen.

Carl was a bright boy from a good family. His roommate, Phil, was a "wiseacre" with a chip on his shoulder and long sideburns. Each morning at 5:45 A.M., Carl would rise, say his prayers to the god of his parents' choice, and jump into a cold shower. By 7:30 his shined shoes found him finishing his scholarship job hosing off things in the bio lab, and ready to enjoy his day of classes with a full binder and no visiting with his neighbor.

Phil never studied, thought campus leaders were "nose-polishers," and rarely woke before noon—although the way his shirttail and long sideburns flapped in the breeze, no one knew if Phil was ever really awake at all!

For Phil had a *bad attitude,* something that goes hand in hand with smart remarks, poor posture, and improper programs of personal hygiene.

At graduation, Carl received a *summa cum laude* for his fine thesis on "Good Posture in Ancient Turkey," and Phil barely squeaked by with mumbled excuses, "borrowed" homework, and long sideburns.

Carl became an important atomic hygienist for the government—Phil drifted from job to job, his long sideburns following him around like two Communist sympathies. After a few years, Carl lost touch with Phil, except for an occasional postcard boasting of smart remarks made to employers and coworkers.

Then, while riding his limousine back from an important business luncheon, Carl noticed a shabby figure polishing gym shoes on the corner. Needing a shine before an important game of business squash, Carl told his chauffeur to pull over. Carl endured strangely familiar mumbled smart remarks (along with a pretty sloppy polishing job) and, as he drove off, he wondered why the remarks seemed to follow him through the traffic....

When Carl stepped from his limousine, he found at his feet something that looked like a freshly dressed side of beef. Seeing no A&P truck nearby, Carl bent over the side of beef and went through its shabby pockets. In its wallet, Carl found no spending money, but he *did* find Phil's dishonorable discharge from the Korean War.

Suddenly, Carl realized what had happened—as his limousine had driven off, the door had slammed shut on one of Phil's sideburns and had dragged him three miles through the midtown rush hour.

Good grades or long sideburns and death—the choice is yours.

The end,

Dean Vernon Wormer

FRATERNITY LIFE AT FABER...

Omega Theta Pi, Faber's Oldest Fraternity

There's more to college life than classes. There's friendship, loyalty, brotherhood, social events, manly virtue, all-night "bull" sessions, a feeling of belonging, high ideals, and dressing right.

At Faber we call it the *Greek system*.

When I joined the fraternity of my choice (as do 80 percent of all male freshmen), I was welcomed into a group of great guys just like me, only *better*, because now there were fifty of us. But frat men are also individuals, too—something that never looks bad on your permanent record.

Soon, you will be "rushing," visiting all of Faber's fraternities to choose the one that's right for you. Which is the best house on campus? Well, Omega House, my own fraternity, *does* have more than its share of campus leaders. But this is not to say that Omega is necessarily for you, depending on who you are.

To be brutally frank, some of you will not make Omega, or any of Faber's fine fraternities. Loners, "party boys," and those who think "individualism" means "being different" need not apply.

A great man once said, "Friendship spawned of true brotherhood in honor canst not gainsay itself against all others."

I believe this is true.

Fraternally yours,

Gregg Marmalard
President, Panhellenic Council

R.O.T.C. AT FABER...

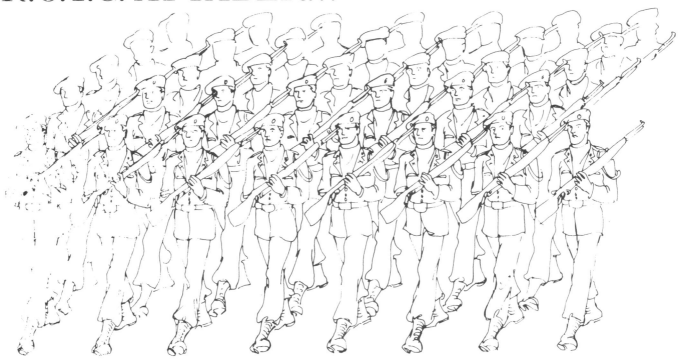

Many freshmen think they enter an "ivory tower" when they begin college. These young men need only climb that tower and look *ninety miles off our coastline* at Communist Cuba to dispel these illusions.

The Soviets would never H-bomb a small campus like Faber, many freshmen think. They should talk to their frat brothers from Nagasaki State, class of '45. But it's too late.

They're all dead.

The Reserve Officer Training Corps at Faber offers students valuable training in leadership, punishment, and military neatness—qualities he will need *after* his period of service, whether he chooses to be a company manager, a corporate executive, or simply go into business.

The U.S. Army needs dedicated young men to protect our campus against real or simulated nuclear attack, supervise Homecoming activities, and run ROTC Day. We build *men*, not fuzzy-thinking one-worlders, and give each cadet an idea of what it's like to risk death in defense of his country—before he really has to.

I am especially proud of the Faber Pershing Rifles, our elite corps of precision killers who, alone, possess the right to wear the shining silver helmet and impressive gold braid, on the battlefield and in the cafeteria.

If you are man enough, and know what I mean by that, feel free to drop in this week at an informal "open house" to meet the other cadets.

Doug Neidermeyer

Douglas C. Neidermeyer
Student Commander
Faber College ROTC

EXTRACURRICULAR ACTIVITIES...

Mandy Peppridge and Barbara "Babs" Jansen

Just because the Faber Mongols football team brings in more money for the college than all student fees, fines, and tuitions combined, that doesn't mean there aren't other things for you to do. Cheerleading, frank-and-program vending, the marching band, or the Mongol Booster Club—each has a place for anyone not good enough to play football or a girl.

"Co-ed" at Faber means just that. Co-ed. Going to classes right alongside the boys, studying right next to sharp Omegas (and boys from Faber's other fine fraternities) until library curfew, cheering the boys good enough to play football. Chatting, laughing, dancing with them, and polishing their footballs. Healthy social relaxation under the tightest adult supervision outside a real correctional facility.

Have fun! And lots of pep! We, too! Sharp.

Mandy Peppridge
Cheerleader Captain

Babs Jansen
Pepsquad Leader

AN INFORMAL HELLO
FROM THE MAYOR...

I want to take this opportunity to welcome you, the class of '66, to Faber, Pennsylvania. Ever since Faber College began, the town of Faber has been right behind it. Sometimes my good friend, the Dean Wormer, jokes about "town and gown" rivalry. But I just kid back and say, "Your campus police have no guns. Mine do."

Then we laugh.

But seriously, the town and the college rely on each other in many ways. *We* pick up your garbage. *We* sell you pizza, movies, and Oldsmobiles. *You* stay on your side of the wall after curfew and nobody gets hurt. Just a good education, okay?

Okay.

Hit the books,

Carmine DePasto
Carmine DePasto
Mayor of Faber

A QUICK HISTORY
OF FABER COLLEGE

FABER COLLEGE was founded in 1904 by Emil Faber, philanthropist and father of the modern American lead pencil. The campus, nestled in the beautiful Saguatashog river valley, was once the site of the original Faber Pencil Works. The pencil mill was built in Faber because of the town's happy proximity to a natural graphite quarry, forests of virgin pencilwood trees, and plentiful wild eraser-root.

As the vogue for lead pencils grew, Emil Faber prospered. Now rich and powerful, he still regretted never having received a college diploma. Thus he funded the construction of FABER COLLEGE in the town he founded, and was soon granted an honorary doctorate in education from the college which, then as now, bears his name, Faber.

FABER FALL STUDENT CALENDAR

SEPTEMBER

16-23	STUDENTS AND PARENTS ARRIVE ON CAMPUS
24-28	FRESHMAN ORIENTATION WEEK
26	LEAF-RAKING DAY
29	FABER MONGOLS VS. NORTH CENTRAL WOMBATS (HOME)

OCTOBER

1	DRESS-UP DAY
3	SORORITY CUPCAKE PAGEANT
5	BLOOD DAY
5	FRESHMAN MIXER—McMACKERAL HALL MUSIC BY JOHNNY AND THE HURRICANES
6	FABER MONGOLS VS. STATE-POLY SLIPSTICKS (AWAY)
11	JEWISH HOLIDAY
12	SOCK HOP—BUMNER GYMNASIUM
13	FABER MONGOLS VS. PURDUKE (HOME)
15	CLEAN SHIRT/BLOUSE DAY
17	PLEDGE HUMILIATION NIGHT
19	FRATERNITY PHONE BOOTH-STUFF FOR FREEDOM
20	FABER MONGOLS VS. APPALACHIA STATE(AWAY)
21	STUDENT SLAVE AUCTION
22-26	MIDTERM EXAM WEEK
27	FABER MONGOLS VS. PARSONS COLLEGE— EXHIBITION (AWAY)

NOVEMBER

2-4	HOMECOMING WEEKEND
2	BONFIRE
3	HOMECOMING PARADE
3	FABER MONGOLS VS. FARLEIGH RIDICULOUS (HOME)
3	HOMECOMING BALL—GEEZNER BALLROOM MUSIC BY SY ZENTNER ORCHESTRA
5-10	SHINED SHOE WEEK
10	FABER MONGOLS VS. SOUTH ALTOONA STATE HUNS (AWAY)
12-19	STUDENT COMPETITION WEEK
22	INTRAFRATERNITY TRICYCLE OLYMPICS

DECEMBER

10-21	FINAL EXAMS
22	CHRISTMAS VACATION

Rush Week

Rush week was not fun. No member of Faber's eight fraternities or four sororities would have disagreed with that. "Odious but necessary" was the kindest thing anyone would say about it. "Pain in the ass" more commonly expressed it for most. And if it was no fun for the upperclassmen, for the incoming freshman boys, two hundred strong, rushing meant a week of horrible, gnawing anxiety. Because at Faber College in 1962, you joined a fraternity or dated women with moustaches and dog breath for four years. Without a house – even if you did find someone nice to go out with – there was nowhere to go. The town of Faber, which adjoined the lovely, verdant campus, was full of factories and mills, and smelled like wet, moldy paper. The street meat scene was limited and fiercely patrolled by guys with engineer boots, pomade, and heavy leather belts. And outside Faber was... what? Fields. A silo. So getting into a fraternity was the absolute top-priority item on every freshman's list during his first few weeks in college. The catch was that not everyone would make it; only about 120 openings existed. What if, even the hottest of high school hot shits was asking himself quietly, in the secret places of his heart – what if maybe I *am* an asshole?

Meanwhile, on Fraternity Row, the seniors were rolling their eyes with collegiate world-weariness. They'd been through this thing three times already, would graduate soon, and didn't have to give a crap. They had other things on their minds. They resented having to put on suits and ties and name tags and spend five nights of their busy, enjoyable lives making inane conversation with nervous young strangers. The sophomores and juniors weren't looking forward to it either, but they *did* have to give a crap. They'd be hanging around with whoever they selected for membership for the next two and three years. So the sophomores and juniors prodded the seniors into a semblance of action and spiffed up their houses and raked their lawns and hung out their colorful, custom-made fraternity flags. By the second Monday after the opening of school, rush week was ready to begin.

* * *

At seven-thirty that evening, in his tiny freshman dorm room, Larry Kroger '66 knotted and reknotted his tie, trying to get the dimple right. He wished he were in Tahiti, or even Philadelphia; anywhere but Faber. He wanted very much to join a frat, but he sure didn't feel like going through the week. He felt as if a dozen volleyballs were dancing the twist in the pit of his stomach. What if he had a diarrhea attack in the middle of talking to some senior fullback? That could definitely happen. "So, Kroger, thinking about being a Sigma, eh?" the fullback would ask him. "Quick! Where's the bathroom?" Larry would reply. Boy, was he going to make a hit out there!

"Ready to go, Lar?" Kent, Larry's roommate of two weeks, dumped his shoeshine stuff in a drawer and put on his sports coat. Kent looked like a potato. He also looked like a shmoo with a double chin and a perspiration problem. There were probably a lot of fat, shapeless things Kent looked like, but Larry hadn't taken it beyond the potato/shmoo stage at this point. All in all, his roommate seemed pretty out of it, though he obviously meant well and certainly was eager to be friends. Larry guessed he liked him well enough; Kent just needed a little help sometimes.

The boys emerged from their dorm into the pleasant autumn night. A full moon hung to one side of the library tower and a little wind rustled the leaves in the trees. Kent forged ahead; a long streamer of toilet paper trailed from the rear of his sports coat like a tail. Larry tugged it free, shaking his head. He wondered briefly if going from house to house with such as Kent Dorfman was the best possible move for him. But then, Kent was the only person he knew in his short time at Faber, and he really couldn't face the prospect of rushing by himself. They passed Johnson Hall. Before it stood the beloved statue of the college founder, Emil Faber, the pencil magnate, with his muttonchop whiskers and lofty bearing. Across the statue's chest some wag had scrawled, "Rushing eats it!" Right, thought Larry. They cut behind Rollins Chapel, turned left on School Street, and arrived on Fraternity Row just as the bells in the library tower struck eight.

The Row was a broad, pleasant thoroughfare lined with stately trees. Handsome, three-story mansions stood on both sides of the street, brightly lit with exterior spotlights. From each fraternity thrust a flagpole supporting an identifying Greek letter flag. Small groups of freshman boys went from frat to frat. Around the corner, on Sorority Row, much the same scene was unfolding for the females of Faber. There was little horseplay. Tension charged the air.

The first house Larry and Kent came to was the most imposing on the Row. Green was its lawn; proud and white were the pillars which formed the three great arches of its broad front porch. Its flag, crisply snapping in the evening breezes, presented in jet black on vivid red the Greek letters *omega theta pi*. Larry had planned to use part of his first two weeks at school to research the various frats, but he'd never gotten around to it. Kent, whose father and older brother had gone to Faber, knew a little more. Omega House, he had said, was "very important." Well, this was

it. He exchanged a nervous glance with Kent, and they headed up the walk.

All at once, Larry realized that Kent was wearing his freshman beanie. "Hey, take that off." Larry snatched it from his head. The beanies were awful looking things.

"But... we're supposed to wear them till Homecoming!" Kent protested.

"Don't be a fruit, okay?" Larry put the beanie inside his jacket and wielded the heavy, omega-shaped door knocker. Kent whisked his jacket open and sniffed each armpit quickly, then brought both hands to his mouth for a hasty breath check.

The door opened. They found themselves facing a tall, broad-shouldered, mean-looking guy in a Madras sports coat, red carnation, and crew cut. His eyes narrowed as he scrutinized them. Then he smiled, a large, white smile, without warmth. "Hi, there. Doug Neidermeyer, Omega rush chairman." He held out a hand.

Larry took it. "I'm Larry Kroger," he said, stepping inside. And this is my..."

"Gah!" cried Kent. Doug had released the door as soon as Larry was in; Kent's head was now trapped between door and sill.

"Oh, excuse me," Doug purred, pulling the door open again. Kent walked in, rubbing his neck sorrowfully.

"...my roommate, Kent Dorfman," Larry finished.

An expression of distaste competed fleetingly with Doug's smile. The smile won and he shook Kent's, hand briefly. "Hi, there. Doug Neidermeyer. And these are our name tag hostesses, Mandy Peppridge and Babs Jansen."

The name tag hostesses were seated at a card table in the vestibule. Larry caught his breath. Both hostesses were knockout blondes. Mandy Peppridge especially was one of the most incredibly good-looking girls he'd ever seen, with golden hair, a beautiful smile, and a pert, upturned nose. Babs Jansen was almost as good-looking as Mandy, but there was something about her skin.... Larry couldn't quite place it.

Mandy wrote out the tags and Babs stood to pin them on the boys' lapels. "Hi there, Kent." She had a strong Southern accent, so it came out, "Hah there. Kay-yunt." She pinned on his tag. "Hi there, Larry. Welcome to Omega House."

Abruptly it came to Larry. Babs Jansen's skin had the texture of a rubber tub toy. "Hi," he said to her. "Nice to meet..."

"Why don't we just go in and meet some of the guys?" suggested Doug. He placed a firm hand on each boy's shoulder and moved them toward the living room. The girls watched them go, then looked at each other.

"A wimp... and a blimp!" said Babs. They burst into giggles.

The Omega living room, with its wood paneling, leather armchairs, and heavy drapes, was the very picture of an exclusive men's club lounge. A fire crackled in the fireplace; hunting prints adorned the walls. Negroes in crisply-starched white waiter jackets were circulating unobtrusively with trays of canapés. In a corner, behind a grand piano, an Omega brother wove dreamily over the keys, emitting a florid interpretation of Pat Boone's "April Love."

Many quiet conversations were in progress. The Omegas seemed all to be extremely well-dressed; the guys you saw each year in the *Esquire* back-to-college fashion layout came to mind. They had wonderfully straight, white teeth and terrific posture. They spoke to the many freshman hopefuls in the crowded room, often laughing knowingly or nodding with gravity.

"Now there's a lot of great guys here tonight, so don't feel you have to meet everybody We just want you to enjoy yourselves while you're here." Doug was guiding them

smoothly through the living room; he smoked a cigarette through a short ivory holder, nodded occasionally to some of the other brothers. When they reached a sofa at the far end of the room, he stopped.

"Hi there, fellas."

Four seated freshmen looked up hopefully – an African kid with tribal marks on his cheeks, horn-rimmed glasses, and a three-piece suit; an extremely skinny boy with a huge nose and no chin, wearing a yarmulke; some sort of exchange student with a black moustache and a turban; and, parked beside the sofa, a blind boy in a wheelchair.

"Fellas, this is Lonnie and Ken," said Doug, moving Larry and Kent to an untenanted section of the sofa. "Lonnie, Ken, I'd like you to meet Clayton, Sidney, ah... Mohamet, and Dave. Just grab a seat, make yourselves at home, and, hey, don't be shy about helping yourselves to the punch and cookies." Giving them a wink, Doug glided away and was lost in the crowd. Larry and Kent exchanged nervous glances with their couchmates.

"Where's my beanie?" demanded Kent. Larry gave it to him, and Kent, looking defiant, put it back on his head.

* * *

Gregg Marmalard, president of Omega, was feeling very much on top of things. With his pinmate Mandy sitting next to him, his tweed jacket that fit him perfectly, and his briar pipe in his mouth, he felt that he looked just about right. The brothers were certainly looking good, too, and they were getting a good rush, even larger than last year's, if he wasn't mistaken. But Omega always had a good rush. It was a house tradition to skim the cream of the incoming freshman class, and this year was proving to be no exception. Take the boy he was talking to right now, Chip Diller. Chip had the right sort of family and wore the right sort of clothes. He even had the right kind of haircut, JFK-style, like his own. Gregg really admired JFK. What was more, Chip had been captain of his prep school tennis team and chairman of its student disciplinary council. Definitely Omega material. It was time, Gregg felt, to see if Chip would commit.

"Now, I'm not going to say that Omega is the *best* house, Chip, but a lot of outstanding guys figure they'll pledge Omega or they won't pledge at all."

Mandy took her cue. "And though Gregg would never tell you this himself, *I* can tell you that there isn't a girl on campus who'd pass up a date with an Omega."

Gregg squeezed Mandy's hand and smiled modestly. "Well, we do have more than our share of campus leaders – something that never looks bad on your permanent record, eh, Chip?"

As far as Chip was concerned, he was ready to sink Omega right now. He felt right at home here. He was about to tell Gregg as much when he suddenly became aware of hot breath on the back of his neck. He turned and found an extremely fat boy in a freshman beanie, smiling eagerly, sweating. Chip felt offended. Maybe he'd better hold up a minute on committing, and see what sort of reception an unpleasant-looking person such as this would receive here.

"Well, sure," he said to Gregg, "everyone I talk to says Omega's the best, but..." He glanced pointedly at the fat boy. "Well, I'd hate to seem *pushy*, you know?"

Gregg put a hand on Chip's shoulder and spoke confidentially. "Listen, Chip, let the unacceptable candidates worry about that, because after tonight, they're..." At Mandy's nudge, he looked up suddenly and beheld the sweating fat boy. Swallowing with annoyance, he looked at the boy's name tag. "You are, uh... Kent." He stood. "I'm Gregg Marmalard and I'd like you to meet my friends, Mandy Peppridge and Chip Diller."

Kent shook hands excitedly. He was all ready with one of his best conversational gambits – "What are you majoring in?" – when Gregg took him firmly by the arm and led him away from Chip and Mandy.

"Have you talked to many of the guys?" Gregg asked. "There's Brother Niedermeyer. I guess you met him at the door. I wonder if you knew that he's student commander of Faber's ROTC?"

"No kidding!" said Kent. "*I'm* in ROTC." He threw a wave to Doug. Doug stared at him.

"And over there is Terry Auerback, captain of the swim team." Gregg vaguely indicated a very tall, dark, handsome, broad-shouldered, wealthy-looking guy in a blue blazer. "And that's Carl Phillips, editor of the *Daily Faberian*." He nodded in the direction of a short, blond, energetic, serious-faced, wealthy-looking guy in a sports coat and turtleneck. "And, ah, this is Clayton, Sidney, Mohamet, Larry, and Dave."

Kent realized with a start that they were back at the rear sofa. Larry looked glumly up at him.

"We've already met," Kent told Gregg hastily.

"Swell! Then you'll have *lots* to talk about." Gregg released Kent's arm and moved off through the crowd. Kent's shoulders slumped. He took a handful of cookies from the tray of a passing Negro, sat down, and began to eat.

* * *

In the next two hours, Larry and Kent visited six more fraternities. Larry felt tired and depressed. Rush was living up to his worst expectations. What was he doing here?

"This is ridiculous," he told Kent. "I don't think any of these houses are going to invite us back. Are we doing something wrong?"

"I dunno, Lar. You're not trying very hard."

Larry kicked at a pebble on the sidewalk. "I hate this."

"Well, listen, no sweat. Remember, I told you my brother was a Delta here. That makes me a legacy. They *have* to take *me*. It's like their law. I'll put in a good word for you, too."

"Great. I hear Delta's the worst house on campus."

Kent sniffed his armpits again and frowned.

"Well, according to the map, it should be right here." Larry was consulting his freshman orientation booklet. "But..."

Before them loomed a house that looked nothing like the others they'd seen that night. There wasn't even a lawn. The front yard was an expanse of dirt, littered with automobile wrecks, empty metal beer kegs, anonymous rusted machine sections, and general, basic garbage. Across the front walk lay a window dummy, nude, female, with no nipples on its understated breasts. On the mannequin's tummy, scrawled in black crayon, was the message, "Just ugly rumors, pal."

The house itself was in an advanced state of blight. Several windows were boarded up, the porch sagged, a pillar leaned dangerously. On the second floor, to the left side, was a great, charred, blackened area, as if from a re-

cent fire. A shopping cart full of empty beer bottles sat by the front door. All that was missing was a sign in front saying CONDEMNED.

There was a good deal of noise coming from inside, however, including some loud rock 'n' roll.

Larry and Kent exchanged a look, shrugged, and headed up the walk. As they neared the porch, they heard a deep, unsteady voice, singing along with the music.

"Louie Louie, whoa whoa, get her way down low," grunted the voice.

The boys could now make out a shadowy figure hefting a beer stein. The guy was facing into a hedge, with his back to them. Kent tapped him timidly on the shoulder.

"Excuse me, sir. Is this the Delta house?"

"Mmmm?" The figure whirled drunkenly. There was a sound, a sort of *fwip-fwip fwip-fwip*, and Larry felt something warm against his legs. He and Kent looked down, astonished, to find that a ragged wet line had just been peed across their neatly-pressed chinos.

The guy smiled. "Hose job!" he announced, sounding surprised but pleased.

He was tremendously squat and dense, with heavy brow ridges and a shock of unruly dark hair. He had a three-day growth of beard and a glint of animal cunning in his eyes. He looked more like a Neanderthal than any other person Larry had ever seen. A smudged name tag pinned to his soiled athletic jacket identified him as BLUTO.

"Sure, this's Delta House," Bluto told them genially, zipping up his fly. "C'mon in." He staggered up the steps with a strange, clumsy grace and pushed through the front door, gesturing broadly for Larry and Kent to follow him. The boys stepped inside.

These things happened: a beer bottle streaked by Larry's head and struck the wall with a crash. "Louie Louie" beat against their ears. A girl ran up in a dress that barely passed her crotch, snatched Kent's beanie from his head, and rushed off, giggling. People whooped and hollered. Bluto plucked another hurled beer from the air and drank half of it in a gulp. "Grab a brew," he told Kent and Larry. "Don't cost nothin'."

The boys stared around in amazement. No other house they'd visited tonight had been remotely like this. People were screaming and laughing and drinking beer. There wasn't a necktie in sight. Piles of pizza and six-packs of Bud formed a small mountain atop the rudely-crafted roulette wheel table in the center of the room. A Frankenstein poster and pictures of half-nude women were on the walls. Four drunk guys at a card table were playing poker using pepperoni slices from the pizza as chips.

Not a few of the rushing freshmen wore expressions ranging from uncertainty to censure. You weren't supposed to drink *beer* at these things. Rushing was serious; it had expressly said so in their orientation booklets.

Larry felt a smile come over his face. "Let's look around," he said to Kent.

They were immediately separated in the swirling tides of the living room. Larry shook his head. The Delta brothers were some of the strangest-looking guys he'd ever seen. For instance, there was a tall, skinny brother with glasses, an overbite, three ballpoint pens clipped to his shirt, and – most interestingly – a leather case hanging from his belt containing a slide rule, strapped to his thigh with a strip of rawhide as if it were a gun in a holster. His name tag said STORK.

"She was up on the piano and down to her underwear," Stork was telling a couple of freshmen. "I about had a cow. Then she took off her..." His voice became lost in the general din.

Now that he noticed it, all the Delta brothers seemed to have colorful, one-word names. Larry saw tags reading BUG, HYDRANT, EINSWINE, COYOTE, and SNOT. He found himself drawn to a small knot of freshmen listening to a large, jolly brother named MOUNTAIN, who was holding forth energetically beneath a moosehead with a missing antler, waving his beer around for emphasis so that occasional pseudopodia of brew had to be ducked. The freshmen were staring at him, fascinated.

"Here's another one," Mountain said. "Confirmed and documented by Cuntwolf, class of fifty-five. It seems the Wolf was dating this Emily Dickinson girl named Barbara Batbreath. Great in the rack but she used to fart all the time. Strange, right? So one night Cuntwolf and Barbara were out at the Rainbow Motel and..."

Kent, meanwhile, had wandered up to the cardplayers' table. Someone had handed him a beer and a piece of pizza, and he felt grateful both for the food and the attention. These Deltas seemed much less aloof than the guys at the other houses. He watched the four card-playing Deltas, smiling hopefully, trying to get their attention. But the cardplayers were totally oblivious to him. In fact, they seemed oblivious to everything but their game. A bottle whizzed between the heads of two of them and smashed loudly against a radiator. None of them blinked.

"Hi, guys," Kent ventured.

"Bump you ten," said the cardplayer named HARDBAR. He threw some pepperoni slices onto the pile in the middle of the table.

"You guys playing cards?"

"Twenty to me?" said BB. "Make it ten more."

"Is this poker?"

"Fold," said DUMPTRUCK.

"How do you play?" Kent asked eagerly.

All four cardplayers turned slowly to look at Kent. Kent beamed at them. The cardplayers stared at him, expressionless. Kent made small, meaningless gestures with his hands and began to shuffle his feet. The cardplayers stared. Kent began backing away. "See you guys later..." But they had already turned back to their game. Kent decided to go find his beanie.

"...and when the Wolf pulled out, there was a piece of tomato and an onion ring sticking to his dong!" Mountain roared at his own story, causing further wholesale sprayings of beer. Of the four freshmen standing with Larry, one's jaw dropped, two turned white, and the fourth walked away rapidly. Larry laughed; he'd thought the story very funny. Almost unbelievably sick, but very funny. He realized that, for the first time all evening, he was enjoying himself. He decided to get a beer.

Mountain directed him to the basement, where the tap system was. Painted on the red walls of the narrow stairwell was a mural depicting a tangle of many bodies – legs, breasts, arms, buttocks, smiling women's faces, and, in the key biological roles, a monkey and a lizard. Scrawled in one corner was "Sod Heap II" and a signature, "Hyena-Class of '57." The basement barroom contained more art – great scrawled signatures and pungent phrases across the ceiling beams and a big yellow delta symbol in the center of the red stone floor. Three pinball games stood against one wall. In a nook to Larry's right was the source of the music, a beat-up Rockola jukebox from which currently blared "Sea Cruise." The bar was across the room and Larry went to it, threading his way through the high-spirited crowd.

Behind the bar, refilling beers for the clamoring masses, was a girl wearing a blue workshirt, nicely tight jeans, and a Delta fraternity pin. Presumably she was the girlfriend of one of the

brothers. She was very pretty, dark-haired with large, lively eyes and a spray of freckles across her nose. Larry liked her instantly. Her name tag said KATY.

"Hi," Larry said.

Katy brushed the hair out of her eyes and glanced at his name tag. "Hi, Larry. Want a beer?" She looked tired and a little tense, Larry thought.

"Sure."

Katy tilted the beer cup beneath the spiggot and deftly flicked the tap. Every imaginable beer sign and bar accessory adorned the area, including the beautiful, hypnotic Miller display with the bouncing, color-shifting balls of light. But most striking of all, on the wall directly behind the bar was a large, cutout painting of a beautiful mermaid with great, globular breasts. The breasts were fishbowls, each containing a small school of lazily swimming goldfish.

Katy returned with his beer. "Nice fish, huh?"

Larry laughed. An extremely tall Delta in a rumpled three-piece suit bustled over to them. He looked kind of like a giant bunny. He took Larry's hand and shook it enthusiastically.

"Welcome to Delta House, Larry. I'm Bob Hoover, house president. Ah... Katy have you seen Boon?"

Katy drew a beer for herself. "He disappeared the minute we got here," she said sourly.

"Probably talking to Otter, I guess," said Hoover.

"No doubt." Katy looked at Larry. "They're well-known homosexuals, you know."

"Ah-ha-ha," Hoover choked. "Have another beer, Larry. Katy's just kidding.' He turned to Bluto, who had just sidled up. "Right, Bluto?"

"Sure." Bluto belched and smashed an empty beer can against his forehead, flattening it. A feverish James Brown side came onto the jukebox.

* * *

Three stories up, in Otter's room, all you could hear of the jukebox music was the throb of the electric bass line, which infused the very walls of Delta House whenever a record was on. Even now, Otter could hear a new bass line beginning. He looked up from his shaving. "Fats Domino?" he asked Boon.

"James Brown. 'You Got the Power.' Nineteen fifty-nine." Boon was the Delta social chairman and record aficionado.

"You got the ear, Boon." Otter rinsed the lather from his face and began expertly to trim the hairs in his nostrils.

Boon regarded his best friend moodily. Life was so simple for Otter. It wasn't just that he was tall, handsome, rich, and had a cherry-red Corvette, though these things didn't hurt. No, it was Otter's simpler world view Boon was thinking about, specifically that all it took to keep Otter completely happy was for him to get regularly laid. And since there was no one at Faber better at getting laid than Otter, he was always happy. His very room looked like a *Playboy* pad, like the ones shown in the magazine each month; it contained a component hi-fi system, a fancy bar stocked with the best liquor, closets and drawers containing Otter's large, impeccable wardrobe, and a sleeping nook decorated with mirrors and fake leopard skin. Good old Otter – the assman's assman.

As for Boon, what made him happy was having fun. Fun *could* mean getting laid, which Boon certainly enjoyed as much as the next guy, but it also could mean a number of other things. Getting incredibly drunk with the guys, for instance, and participating in some kind of horror show. Or, getting incredibly drunk with the guys and listening to obscure rhythm and blues records all night. And then there was getting incredibly drunk with the guys and telling sick stories back and forth until they all passed out. Boon's tastes were more catholic than Otter's. Until recently, his pinmate Katy had seemed to enjoy all the same activities he did. What a perfect Delta girlfriend she'd been all last year, hanging out nightly at the tap system with him, drinking as well as any of the brothers; she'd been his female alter ego. Only this year something was wrong. Christ, he'd hardly been able to get her to come down to the house tonight for as important an occasion as rushing. Boon sighed. Well, maybe things would get better as the school year got seriously underway. He looked up at his friend. Otter, in his snap towel, was still

before the mirror, getting his part just right. He was whistling "Peter's Theme" from *Peter and the Wolf*, which usually meant he was about to dive into some co-ed's pudding.

"Otter, what's the story? You gotta date tonight?"

Otter smiled.

Boon laughed. The Delta rush chairman was going out on a date on the first night of Rush Week. "Who? Norma?"

"No, but I'll give you a hint: she has a couple of major league yabbos." Otter cupped his hands before his chest as if hefting great masses.

"Beverly!"

"You're getting closer. Here's another hint." Otter rolled his eyes up, let his mouth go slack, and squealed in falsetto, "You're *in* me, you're *in* me, oh God, I can *feel* you..."

"Marlene? What? Don't tell me you're gonna pork Marlene Desmond?"

Otter winced. "Pork?"

Boon felt obscurely annoyed. Maybe it was envy. Marlene Desmond was gorgeous and made no demands. "You're gonna hump her brains out, aren't you, you insatiable scumbag."

"Boon, I anticipate a deeply religious experience." Otter went to the sweater drawer and selected a red V-neck. "Anyway, what's this great interest in my social life? Where's Katy?"

Boon looked glum. "Downstairs. I think she's pissed off about something."

Otter slipped into his gray sports jacket. "Says you're an immature jerk, eh?"

"Yah. I don't take anything seriously."

Otter, fully dressed and groomed now, and, Boon had to admit, resplendent as ever, went to the bar and took out

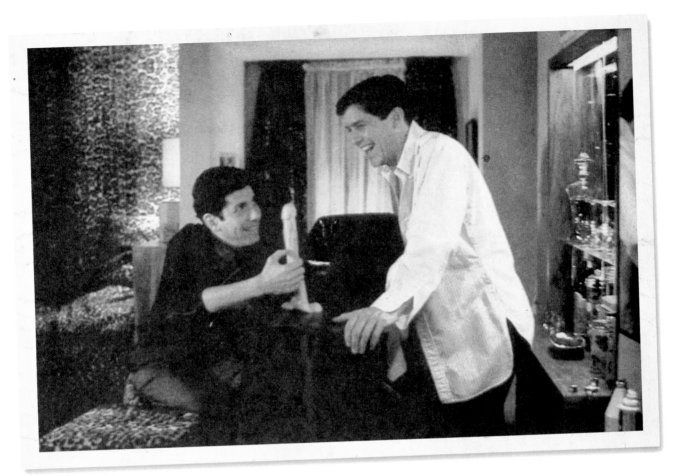

his genuine leather doctor's bag, a collection of sexual apparatus and accessories he called his "traveling kit." He opened the bag and withdrew a long, penis-shaped dildo. It was made from some kind of rubber that looked like skin and even had anatomically correct veins entwining it. Otter proffered the thing to Boon.

"She'd take this seriously. Try it."

Boon eyed it dubiously. He took it from Otter and ventured a couple of swings with it, as if it were a baseball bat. "Louisville slugger?"

"Coney Island wife-tamer."

The door opened suddenly and Hoover stuck his head into the room. "Are you guys coming down? I mean, really, it's ten o'clock and you haven't even..."

"Sorry, Hoov," said Otter. "Gotta date."

Hoover blinked. "But... you're supposed to be rush chairman!"

"You know I can't handle responsibility."

Hoover couldn't believe it. "Then why did you run for the job in the first place?"

Otter thought about that for a second. "I don't remember."

Boon laughed. Hoover turned to him beseechingly. "Boon!"

"All right, all right. We're coming."

Boon and Otter, right hands waggling invisible straw hats above their heads, did a vaudeville glide by Hoover into the hall. Sighing, Hoover followed.

Larry, carrying his beer, wandered up to the second floor of the house. He saw Bluto and a skinny, pimply freshman emerge from a doorway. Painted on the door in large letters was SEXROOM.

"So that's where you take 'em when you want to rip off a piece in the house." Bluto gave the freshman a nudge and a sly wink. "Just save some for the rest of us, you crazy stallion." The freshman laughed nervously.

Larry decided to see what the Sex Room looked like, but before he could take a step he heard a tremendous crash from the first floor. A guy on a motorcycle had just smashed open the front door to Delta House and was now headed straight for the stairs. Larry gulped. The guy was going to try to come right *up* the stairs. Several freshmen hurled themselves out of the way as the bike hit the first stair, bounced high off the second, and roared straight at Larry. He flattened himself against the wall, wide-eyed.

The motorcycle came to a full, screeching halt directly in front of him. Larry didn't move; the bike had him totally boxed in. The rider calmly rocked the big Harley onto its kickstand, doffed his World War II helmet, pushed up his goggles, and smiled at Larry.

"What can I say? I'm the hottest thing on wheels."

He was one of the most unusual looking people Larry had ever seen. His haircut was the kind you'd see worn by guys at gas stations – long on the sides, absolutely flat on top, combed back into a ducktail. A thick, jaunty moustache, waxed up into points, adorned his upper lip, giving him the air of a dashing RAF fighter ace. He was clad in an olive-drab flight suit with pockets and zippers everywhere, combat boots, and a pair of grimy leather gloves with all the fingers cut off. His name tag said D-DAY.

D-Day drew a beer from his utility belt, flipped its cap off with the church key hanging from his neck on a dog tag chain, and handed it to Larry. As Larry took it, foam erupted from inside, flowing down the bottle onto his hand. D-Day smiled raffishly drew a second bottle, opened it, thrust the neck in his mouth, and threw his head back, getting all the foam and swallowing much of the rest of the beer in the process. He glanced at Larry. The freshman was regarding him with his mouth open, speechless. D-Day stuffed the beer back into his belt, tilted his chin up and played the "William Tell Overture" in a rapid finger tattoo on the stretched skin of his throat.

Larry broke up laughing.

Looking pleased, D-Day dismounted, clapped Larry on the shoulder, and trotted down the stairs. Larry shook his head. He couldn't believe this place. This was unquestionably the most fun he'd had since arriving at Faber.

* * *

"Certs is a candy mint," declared Boon.

"Certs is a *breath* mint," said Otter.

"Fucking *candy* mint!"

"Breath mint! Breath mint!"

They stopped halfway down the stairs and began strangling each other.

"Candy," snarled Boon.

"Breath," Otter managed to choke out.

"Will you guys cut it out?" said Hoover anxiously. "There are freshmen watching."

"Right, Hoov. Freshmen." Otter let go of Boon, straightened his jacket, and went into the living room, immediately beginning to shake hands with maniacal energy, a grotesquely sincere smile on his face. "Eric Stratton, rush chairman. So *damn* glad to meet you. Hey, Eric Stratton, rush chairman. So damn glad to meet *you*."

Abruptly, he came upon Kent. It was love at first sight.

"Hello," said Kent. "My name's..."

"Say, is that a clip-on, by any chance?" Otter bent to look more closely at Kent's tie. "Boon! Check this out!"

Boon came over. He lifted the tie to read the label. "Mmm, 90 percent rayon. Very nice. You pick this little number up locally?"

"I got it at home," Kent explained, delighted to be talking to somebody.

"You know, you should always wear a beanie," Otter told him. "It makes your head look bigger."

"Thanks!"

Hoover rushed over and put a protective arm around Kent's shoulders. "Kent's a legacy, Otter. His brother is Fred Dorfman, '59."

"He said legacies usually get asked to pledge automatically." Kent looked hopefully from Hoover to Otter.

"Well, usually," said Otter. "Unless, of course, the pledge in question turns out to be a real closet case."

"Yeah. Ha-ha," snorted Kent.

"Please don't do this, Otter," said Hoover under his breath.

Boon looked up and saw Katy in the hallway. She had her coat on, was headed for the door, and was giving him the finger. Boon blinked.

"You know the type, Kent," Otter continued. "Rotund, perspiring, hair like greasy noodles, vague smell of rancid bacon fat hovering in the..."

"Hey, later, you guys," said Boon, heading for the door. What the hell was up with her?

* * *

Katy was already halfway across the front yard. Boon rushed to catch up. "Where you going?"

"Home, Donald."

"But we just got here."

Katy stopped and faced him. She looked furious. "No, Boon. *You* just got here. *I've* been downstairs for two hours, entertaining some kid from Pig's Knuckle, Arkansas."

Boon hated it when Katy got like this. Which had been happening more and more often lately. Well, maybe she was right, maybe they didn't get to spend enough time together, away from the house. He put his arms around her.

"Baby, I'm sorry. Listen, maybe we could drive up to your folks' place this weekend."

Katy shook his arms off. "Fabulous. *My* car full of *your* beer buddies going up to empty *my parents'* liquor cabinet. It's just too depressing to think about."

"No, baby, just maybe Otter and one other girl..."

"Boon, is this really how you're going to spend the rest of your life?"

He looked at her blankly. "What do you mean?"

"I mean hanging around with a bunch of animals, getting drunk every weekend?"

Boon put his arms around her and looked very serious. "No. After I graduate I'm going to hang around with a bunch of animals and get drunk *every night*."

Katy's shoulders slumped. She smiled wanly. "My problem is I'm in love with a retard."

"Right!" said Boon, gesturing wildly. "Guh-hyuck!" He tripped over an old tire and fell sprawling. Katy laughed and helped him up.

Got through another one, thought Boon. Why couldn't this problem with Katy just go away? Well, maybe it still would. Sure, and maybe the moon would fall out of the sky. Oh, well, he'd worry about it later. He put his arm around her and they headed toward her off-campus apartment.

* * *

When rush closed at eleven, Larry and Kent went to Pop's Pizza. Kent ordered a large pie, Larry a coke. They sat down.

"I bet they're not going to take me," said Kent dismally.

Larry watched three teen-age girls walk in and go to the counter to order. They looked like townies. One of them was cute. "I thought they had to take you because your brother was a member."

Kent swallowed a bite of pizza and sighed. "Yeah, but I make a lousy first impression."

"Who told you that?"

"My mother."

Larry turned his attention back to the girls. They were carrying their pie to a table. One of them, the cute blonde, stopped and looked at Larry. She smiled and walked right over to him. Larry felt his throat go tight. He struck a casual pose.

The girl looked about sixteen. She was even prettier up close than she'd been at a distance. She popped her gum and addressed both boys. "Either of you guys twenty-one? That creep won't sell us any beer."

They answered simultaneously.

"Yes," said Larry.

"No," said Kent.

There was a moment of strained silence.

"Well, I am, he's not," said Larry. "Unfortunately, I left my wallet in my room and all my IDs are in it."

Kent chortled through a mouthful of pizza. Larry glared at him.

"Thanks anyway. Maybe some other time." She smiled at Larry and started to turn away.

"Yeah," snorted Kent. "In about three years."

The girl went back to her friends. Furious, Larry gave Kent a hard noogie punch on the arm.

"Hey, *ouch!*" squealed Kent. "What'd *I* do?"

"Engine Manifolds." He wasn't sure what to do next; he couldn't remember a word of the formal Delta pledging ritual.

"Get it over with, cheese dip!" bellowed Bluto.

"Okay, okay." He'd just have to come up with something. "Ah, pledges, repeat after me – I, state your name..."

"I, state your name..." said the pledges.

Hoover looked pained, but went on. "...do pledge allegiance to the frat..."

"...do pledge allegiance to the frat..."

"...with liberty and, ah, fraternity for all."

"...with liberty and fraternity for all."

"Amen," Hoover added.

"Amen."

He shut the book happily, "Gentlemen, let us drink."

A great cheer went up from the brothers. As one man, they shook up their beer bottles and fired them at the pledges; great parabolas of foam blasted the boys. Then the brothers rushed up to drain the rest of their beers directly over the freshmen's heads.

"Yow!" cried Larry.

"Hey!" spluttered Kent happily.

The jukebox exploded into life and the serious drinking began.

* * *

At the far end of the Row, at Omega, pledging ceremonies were also underway. The house was dark, except for the chapter room, where a hundred candles cast a flickering light on the proceedings. The Omega brothers, standing in a semicircle, wore black, cowled robes which afforded only the briefest glimpses of their faces. Before them, in coats and ties, were the ten new Omega pledges, including a proud Chip Diller. Over all hung the giant, blood-red seal of Omega Theta Pi.

"The Omega pledge pin," intoned Gregg Marmalard, holding out a golden chalice full of them. "A simple bronze shield bearing the inscription SEMPER FRATERNITAS, or, 'All men are brothers.' For the special elite who are lucky enough to wear it, let this pin symbolize your pledge of fealty to Mother Omega. Wear it with humble pride. Pledgemaster Neidermeyer?"

Doug took a pledge pin from the chalice and comported it to the lapel of Chip Diller. Chip smiled loftily.

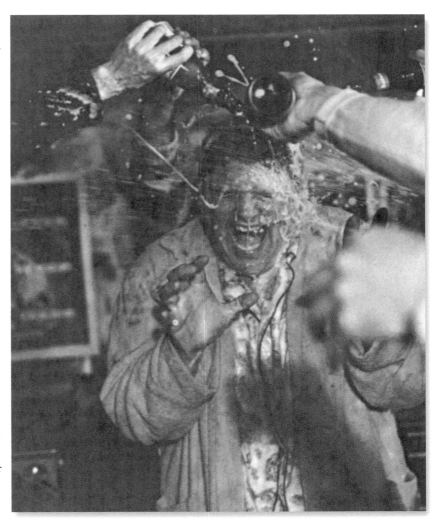

As the new Delta pledges were consuming their first official Delta beers at the bar, Bluto passed among them with a greasy Dixie cup full of pledge pins. "Okay, Pledge Joshua, your Delta name's gonna be Mothball. Because you belong in a closet. Got that?"

The skinny, pimply pledge gulped, nodded, and took the pin.

"What's *my* Delta name gonna be?" asked Kent excitedly.

"A lot of thought went into that one, Dorfman. From now on, you're Flounder."

"Flounder?" Kent tasted the name unhappily.

"Kroger." Bluto handed Larry a pledge pin. "Your Delta name's gonna be Pinto."

Larry looked puzzled. "Why?"

Every brother in the room spun suddenly to face him. *"Because you've got a spotted dong!"* they roared delightedly.

* * *

When the pins were all handed out, the Omega pledges stripped down to their underpants for the next stage of the ritual, and knelt before the brothers. Doug Neidermeyer stepped forward with a broad, heavy pledge paddle.

"We now consecrate the bond of obedience," said Gregg. "Pledge Diller, assume the position."

Chip got up and moved a few steps to stand before Doug. He about-faced, bent over, and grabbed his ankles.

"Pledgemaster, do your duty." Gregg crossed his arms.

Doug raised the paddle. His eyes were very bright and his mouth worked. He smacked the paddle hard against Chip Diller's ass.

Chip winced, but bravely called out, "Thank you, sir, may I have another?"

Whack!

"Thank you, sir, may I have another?"

Whack!

"Thank you, sir, may..."

* * *

Two kegs had already kicked at Delta House, but Boon had immediately replaced them with fresh ones, and the drinking was continuing unabated. Pledgemaster Bluto organized crew races. In this competition, six brothers faced the six new pledges across the bar, each boy with a fresh beer in front of him. Boon started each contest by chugging a beer himself, then slamming the empty glass down on the bar. The first brother and first pledge grabbed their beers, drank them down as fast as they could, and slammed

their glasses onto the bar, signaling the next boys to begin. Essentially, it was a relay race, with the losers expected to drink an additional round as penance. Since Bluto and Stork had the knack of opening their throats and simply pouring the beer down, the brothers hadn't lost a match. The pledges were getting astoundingly shitfaced.

Hardbar, Delta historian, had organized an informal seminar. An enthusiastic loremaster, he also was noted for his frequency of masturbation and love of pinball. As Boon's fellow New Yorker and rock 'n' roll authority, he was the only other member of the house allowed to open up the jukebox and put new records in.

"One of our oldest traditions," he told the pledges, "is 'Kegs instead of paddles.' That's because we feel it's more valuable to the developing individual to be drunk than in pain. Remember, though – we expect you guys to learn how to drink well. And boot well. As an old house expression has it, 'Drink Delta – boot Delta.'"

"What's 'boot'?" asked Flounder, unkempt and blissful.

Bluto stepped up with a full pitcher of beer. "Here's a demonstration." He lifted the pitcher to his mouth and drained three-quarters of it. Setting the pitcher aside, he faced the pledges and held up his right index finger for their inspection. He stuck the finger briefly down his throat.

"Blawwwwwwwwwwwww!" A geyser of beer and foam erupted from Bluto's mouth, lofted over the pool table and struck the far wall with a splat. The pledges stared at him, dumbstruck. Bluto smiled genially at them and calmly took a fresh swallow from the pitcher.

"Now, that was what we call a 'power boot'," Hardbar explained. "Little dispersion, lots of velocity. Bluto's very good at these things."

"I could *never* do that," murmured Flounder, wide-eyed.

"Sure you could," Bluto said encouragingly. "Why not?"

"I've never been able to throw up, even when I was sick." Flounder looked very worried.

Bluto threw a comradely arm around his shoulders. "Mark my words, Flounder: before you leave the Delta House you'll be booting like a pro."

All at once, Boon cranked the sound on the jukebox to peak volume. "Louie Louie" had just come on for the fifteenth time that night, and Boon was moving right into some fancy, choreographed R&B moves.

Louie Louie, whoa no
Baby we gotta go

Bomp bomp
Ya ya ya ya ya ya ya

Otter, Bluto, D-Day, and Hoover joined Boon, picking up the step.

Louie Louie, whoa baby
Get her way down low

The pledges laughed with glee at the antics of the brothers. "Pinto! Flounder!" Boon gestured them over. "C'mon, you're gonna learn this." Pinto and Flounder joined the line of singing brothers uncertainly.

If she's got the rag on
I'll work above
It won't be long
Till she's slippin' it off
Then I'll take her in my arms again
Tell her I'll never ever lay her again

Pinto seemed to be picking up the step pretty well. Flounder couldn't do it at all, but nobody cared. Hardbar and Stork, elated, rushed over and dumped more beer on everyone.

Louie Louie, whoa baby
Get her way down low
Bomp!

BOON
SOCIAL CHAIRMAN

HARDBAR
HISTORIAN

D-DAY
SGT.-AT-ARMS

MOUNTAIN

EINSWINE

BB

𝕯elta 𝕿

19

COYOTE

TURNIP

DOUCHE

FOX

SNOT

PINTO

FLOUNDER

MO

OVER
ESIDENT STORK
TREASURER OTTER
RUSH CHAIRMAN BLUTO
PLEDGEMASTER

Chi

3

RANK ROACH DUMPTRUCK

BUG HOOD MUMBLES GHOUL

L ASSWIPE MOUSE HYDRANT

School Begins

With rushing finally over, the Faber campus heaved a giant, collective sigh of relief and turned to the day-to-day business of classes. The Delta long suit was not academics. Most of the seniors had picked notoriously easy "gut courses," such as Rocks 1, the basic survey geology course, and Nuts 'n' Sluts, known formally as Abnormal Psychology 101. But Pinto had no choice; he took the freshman courses to which he was assigned, and none of them were guts. Pinto found himself in English 1, History 5, French 1, Math 1 (Introduction to Calculus), and Chemistry 5 (Quantitative Analysis). The only one he liked was English, and that was because the prof was cool.

Actually, he wasn't a professor. Mr. Jennings had graduated from Faber some years earlier. As word had it, he had gone to New York and lived in Greenwich Village. Then he'd returned to Faber to get a graduate degree and been made a teaching assistant. Unlike the other profs, who treated their subjects with high seriousness, Jennings often made fun of his material, the school, and himself. All his students agreed; Dave Jennings was very cool.

But even in English class, Pinto's mind kept wandering from the lectures. He had discovered on the Monday after rush week that there was a co-ed seated in the row behind him, a couple of seats to the right, who turned him on incredibly. He watched Mr. Jennings writing on the blackboard, trying to keep his mind on the lecture, but his attention kept straying to the co-ed. She had spectacular, torpedo-like breasts pressing against her sweater, and her skirt was hiked halfway up her thighs.

"John Milton, 1608-1674," said Jennings, printing it on the blackboard. "Now, what can we say about Milton's *Paradise Lost?*" He glanced around the room. Fifty passive freshman faces looked back at him. He sighed. "Well, we can say that it's a very *long* poem; it was written a very long time ago, and I'm sure a lot of you may have difficulty understanding exactly what Milton was trying to say."

In his seat near Pinto, Flounder was scribbling busily in his notebook. He was drawing a beautifully detailed picture of an F-86 Sabre jet attacking a MiG-15 high over the battlefields of Korea. Chip Diller was working a hand exerciser, silently counting the repetitions. Mothball was sleeping.

"Certainly we know he was trying to describe the struggle between good and evil, right?" Again, Jennings looked around the room. He saw no trace of response, so he answered his own question. "Right. And yet who is the poem's most engaging character?" The class stared at him blankly. "Well, don't everyone jump at once. The most 'interesting' character? The most 'fun'? Look, did any of you read this? Because maybe I'm just wasting my time and I should show a film."

The class shifted nervously in their seats and attempted to appear alert. Pinto was checking out the girl again. He decided to try something he'd learned in high school. With extreme casualness, he knocked his ball-point pen on the floor, then bent to pick it up. He pretended to fumble a bit for it, to gain time, and sent his gaze right up the co-ed's skirt. From the zone between her stocking tops and her

black panties, white thigh winked at him. He began to get a hard-on. Sitting up quickly, face flushed, he pressed a textbook down against his lap; he felt faint with desire.

"Okay, as we all know from our reading, the most intriguing character was Satan." Jennings turned to the blackboard and wrote *Satan.* "Now, was Milton trying to tell us that being bad was more fun than being good?" He took an apple from his desk top and bit into it. "Or was he trying to warn us to watch out for snakes because they walk funny?"

The exerciser popped from Chip's sweaty hand and struck his desk with a clatter. He gazed innocently ahead and quickly slipped it in his pocket.

"Okay, don't write this down," said Jennings, "but I find Milton probably as boring as you do. Mrs. Milton found him boring, too. He's a little long-winded, he doesn't translate very well into our generation, and his jokes are terrible...."

The bell rang. Fifty students stood as one and began heading rapidly for the exits.

"But that doesn't relieve you from your responsibility for this material," Jennings called over the noise. "I'm still waiting for reports from some of you. I'm not joking; this is *my job!*" A girl dropped her paper on his desk in passing. "Thanks," he said, surprised.

The last of the students left the room. Or not quite the last. Mothball was still slouched in his front row seat, fast asleep. Jennings took a final bite from his apple and tossed the core at the slumbering boy, caroming it off his head. Mothball blinked and looked around. Gulping, he pulled his books together and rushed out the exit door.

Jennings turned to the board and erased *Satan.* "Jesus," he muttered.

* * *

Dean Vernon Wormer was a scary man. He was fifty, physically large, and had, when angry, a face so mean he looked like he could bite the fender off a car and tear it to pieces with his teeth. As dean of students, it was his duty to see to it that the student body behaved itself, and he was good at his job. If annual intimidation awards had been given at Faber, the dean would have taken the prize the last ten years running.

Yes, Dean Wormer had been highly successful at Faber – with one important exception. And that exception was like a giant, jagged thorn in his side at all times; it had given him three ulcers and he was certain he could feel in his stomach the beginnings of a fourth. If only for the sake of his health, it was time to do something decisive. Which was why Gregg Marmalard, president of the Pan-Hellenic Council, currently sat across his desk from him.

The dean stood and stared out the window. "Gregg, what's the worst fraternity on campus?"

Gregg shifted in his chair. "That'd be hard to say, sir. They're each outstanding in their own way, and..."

"Let's just skip the bullshit, Gregg. I have their disciplinary file right here." He dropped a folder thick as the

London telephone directory on his desk; it landed with a thud.

He opened the folder at random. "Who, in 1955, drove a flock of sheep through graduation ceremonies?" He turned a page. "In '57, who threw a 'surprise pajama party' – and held thirty-seven co-eds in nightgowns captive in their basement for a day and a half?"

He began to leaf faster, his face becoming redder with every page. "The next year, who crated up the statue of Emil Faber and shipped it to Khrushchev? Do you have any idea how much it cost to get it back?" The pages flew before his eyes. "Who dropped a truckload of Fizzies in the swim meet? Who delivered the medical school cadavers to the alumni dinner?" The dean slammed the file closed. "Every Halloween all the toilets explode! Every spring the trees are full of underwear!"

Gregg nodded gravely. "You're talking about Delta, sir?"

"*Yes,* I'm talking about Delta, you jack-off! Who else would…"

The phone rang. Dean Wormer eyed it uneasily. "But this year it's going to be different. This year we're going to…"

The phone rang a second time. Dean Wormer looked agitatedly through the door to his outer office. "Miss Leonard?"

"She's not at her desk, sir."

"Christ on a crutch." The dean picked up the phone. A voice began coming from it instantly. He regarded the receiver unhappily and brought it to his ear. "Hello, Marion."

Pause.

"No, Marion."

Pause.

"Not now, Marion."

Pause.

"You're drunk, Marion. Go back to bed." He set the receiver down, removed his glasses, and massaged the bridge of his nose. Abruptly, he remembered Gregg.

"Now what was I… oh, yes, the Delta House. Gregg, this year we're going to grab the bull by the balls and kick those punks off campus!"

"What do you intend to do, sir? Delta's already on probation."

"They are?"

"Yes, sir."

"Oh." Dean Wormer pounded his fist decisively on his desk. "Then, as of this moment, Delta is on double secret probation!"

Gregg looked confused. "Double secret probation, sir?"

The dean turned to him, wild-eyed. "Get the crud out of your ears, son. There is a little-known codicil in the Faber College constitution that gives the dean unlimited power to preserve order in times of emergencies. Sort of like declaring martial law, only…"

"Double secret." Gregg nodded. "Yes, sir. But I'm still not clear on what you want *me* to do."

The phone rang. The dean looked at it with trepidation. "It's a nice day," he declared. "Let's continue this outdoors."

They left the administration building and strolled along one edge of Faber's green, well-kept central quadrangle. Several touch football games were in progress.

"Gregg, what I want you to do is pull your thumb out of your butt and find me a way to revoke Delta's charter. You're right down the block from them. Put Neidermeyer

on it; he's a sneaky shit like you, right? The time has come for someone to put his foot down, and that foot is me! Do I make myself clear?"

Gregg smiled. "Yes, sir!"

"Good." The Dean noticed a little group of student sitting on the front steps of a dormitory. He smiled and waved cheerily at them. They didn't wave back.

Not far from Gregg and Dean Wormer, on an auxiliary athletic field behind the gym, there was much afternoon activity. At the center of the field the ROTC drill team was going through its moves, while in an end zone, Doug Neidermeyer was breaking in a squad of green freshman cadets. At the far end of the field, the varsity cheerleaders were about to commence their practice.

Mandy Peppridge was in the bleachers tying her sneakers when Babs Jansen ambled over and took a seat next to her. Mandy concentrated on her laces. Of all her Tri Pi sisters, Babs was the biggest snoop. She'd been prying at Mandy regarding her relationship with Gregg since the beginning of the semester, and Mandy was getting sick of it.

But Babs was not to be put off. "Come on, Mandy, honey. You know *I'd* tell *you.* Are you and Gregg doin' the dirty deed or not?"

Mandy gave her a cool look. "Gregg doesn't believe in premarital intercourse."

"Too bad," Babs sighed. "I think he's just dreamy."

"Okay, let's hit it!" Mandy bounced to her feet and ran out to join the rest of the girls.

Directly beneath the bleacher seat Mandy had just left, Bluto leaned back against a grandstand support, sweat dotting his forehead. Right up her cheerleader skirt he had peeked. "Leg," he thought thickly. "Thigh. Box." He

bunched himself forward and peered through the bleachers as the girls went into their first cheer.

We got the pep
We got the steam
We got the coach, team, pep, steam
Fifteen rahs and a yay team!

On *"team,"* Mandy soared skyward in her spread-legged cheerleader leap, waving her pompons furiously. Bluto made soft whimpers.

"Eyes front!" bellowed Doug Neidermeyer. "Don't watch me! What do you think *attention* means?"

The eight freshman cadets stared rigidly straight ahead. Among them was Chip Diller. *His* eyes had never wavered in the first place. He felt contempt for his fellow cadets.

Doug was mounted on the ROTC horse, a great white stallion named Trooper that Doug cared about more than any other living thing at Faber. The cadets, for their part, hated and feared Trooper. The horse was unnaturally mean. Even now, as Doug rode through their ranks, the beast was snapping at their faces and stepping on their feet. They attempted, unsuccessfully, to stand firm.

"You're worthless and weak," Doug bawled. "Drop and give me twenty!"

The freshmen hit the dirt and began doing push-ups. Doug rode among them. "One! Two! Three! Straight backs!" The cadets grunted and strained. "Lift your heads so you can look across the field. You see those men?" He waved his riding crop toward the drill team. Like Doug, they wore silver helmets, orange ascots, and lots of flashy braid at the shoulders. As the freshmen watched, the drill team executed a right oblique, a left oblique, a double about-face, and a Victoria salute.

"Those men are the Pershing Rifles, Faber's finest. And you are..." He broke off as he spotted two uniformed latecomers emerging at a dead run from the concrete tunnel that led to the locker rooms. "At ease, you men!" Doug barked to the cadets, and took off at full gallop.

Pinto and Flounder, winded and very worried, tore across the athletic field.

"Right there!" shouted Doug. "Ten-hut!"

Pinto and Flounder froze. Trooper galloped up to them and spun around, tail high, his ass inches from their faces.

Doug reined him in and eyed the boys with heat. "What time is it, mister?" he asked Pinto.

"I... don't know, sir."

"That's obvious, mister!"

"Sorry, sir," said Flounder, in a voice squeaky with fear. "It was my fault, sir."

Doug stared at Flounder as if he were a pit filled with zoo filth. Everything about the fat freshman's uniform was wrong. His stomach pressed his too-small jacket almost to bursting, and his tie was askew. A large grass stain covered one knee of his trousers. His *underwear* peeped from one side of his belt.

"You fat, disgusting slob! You're a goddamned disgrace!" Doug got off Trooper and thrust his face at Flounder. Flounder began to quiver.

Otter and Boon, with Mothball toting their clubs, set out from the Delta House to play a little golf. Both were dressed in their snazzy golf duds, with colorful, puffy trousers and Ben Hogan caps. They heard Doug Neidermeyer screaming as they were crossing the grassy hill that overlooked the athletic fields.

"Vicious motherfucker, isn't he?" remarked Boon.

"Yeah," said Otter. "He can't do that to our pledges."

Boon nodded. "Right. Only *we* can do that to our pledges." He took his bag from Mothball. Unzipping the pocket, he removed several balls and a tee.

Doug smacked Flounder on the chest with his riding crop. "Redo those buttons." He poked him in the stomach. "Dress that belt buckle." Flounder looked down to comply and Doug knocked off his service cap from behind. "Straighten that cap!" Flounder hastily put the cap back on. "And, god *damn* it, tuck in that underwear!" Neidermeyer ceased his slow, circular prowl around Flounder and froze. "Ten-hut! Eyes front! What's-that-on-your-chest?"

Flounder could barely speak. "It's a pledge pin, sir."

"A *pledge* pin?" Neidermeyer was screaming in the distance. "On your uniform?"

Boon gave a preliminary waggle and teed off. The ball hooked sharply. "Shit," he said.

Doug's face was an inch from Flounder's; his eyes seemed to be boring icy holes through him. Flounder swallowed with great difficulty. "I – I was told to wear it everywhere, sir."

"I see. Just tell me, mister; what fraternity would pledge a man like you?" Doug was so close Flounder could feel the spittle strike him with Doug's every word. "It's a Delta pin, sir."

On the hill, Boon tried again; the ball flipped off to the right. "Slice!" said Boon, disgusted.

"A *Delta* pin," said Doug. "Our worst cadet pledges our worst fraternity. Dorfman, you will report to the stable, tonight and every night, at nineteen hundred hours. And without that pledge pin! *Do you understand?*"

Flounder gulped and nodded.

"Now get into ranks!"

Pinto and Flounder rushed over to the other cadets and fell in at the end of the line. Chip sneered exquisitely as they passed him.

Doug remounted Trooper. "Ten-hut! Right face! Mark time – harch! Fo-ward – harch!"

The line of boys stepped off and began marching across the end zone.

Otter accepted a two-wood from Mothball and teed up. "Your left arm's up, Boon, but you're not keeping your *head* down." He swung; there was a satisfying *smack* and the ball streaked straight toward Neidermeyer.

The white spheroid came out of nowhere and struck Trooper on his left buttock. Doug never saw it arrive; all he knew was that suddenly Trooper was rearing wildly, menacing the line of cadets. The cadets scattered in all directions.

"Easy, boy." Doug struggled to control the crazily bucking animal. "Goddamn it, hold your ranks!" he bawled at the freshmen.

Otter continued his lesson, making a row of tees and placing a ball on each. "Just stay loose and always try to hit *through* the ball." He swung again, and his second drive was nearly identical to his first.

"Trooper! Settle down, big fella!" Doug barked. The horse was still cutting back and forth unpredictably. The second golf ball hurtled in, striking Doug on his gleaming, silvery helmet, which rang like a bell. He looked very surprised, and toppled backward, off the horse, his left foot catching in the stirrup. The horse plunged forward and galloped down the middle of the athletic field.

The cheerleaders were lining up for another cheer, the new one Mandy had devised. "Hit it!" Mandy called, and the girls went into their moves.

Genghis was a Mongol
And Kublai was, too
So look out Polytechnic
'Cause Faber's coming through!

Trooper barreled into their midst. Mandy practically froze at the top of her leap and the other girls hurled themselves out of the way. The horse, still dragging Doug, galloped across a cinder track straight into the tunnel to the locker rooms.

"*Gahhhhhhhhhhhhhhhhhh!*" Doug screamed; the cry took on a surreal, hollow quality as he disappeared, and subsided into echoes.

Otter bagged his club. Mothball stared at him, awed.

"I've got to work on my game," Boon said, as they started down the hill.

Otter shook his head and smiled. "Don't think of it as work. The whole point is to *enjoy* yourself."

"*Gahhhhhhhhhhhhhhhhhhhhhh!*" howled Doug.

The Pershing Rifles spun in amazement to find Commander Neidermeyer's horse bearing down on them, dragging Commander Neidermeyer. They arranged themselves so as to be able to tear him free as the horse made its pass.

Abruptly, hard white missiles began to rain down on them. The impact of balls on helmets made strange music, like a child randomly smiting a xylophone.

"Hey, ouch!" yelled one Pershing Rifle.

"Whut th' hail?" yelped another. "Let's git th' fuck outa hyar!"

The Pershing Rifles sprinted for cover, and Trooper galloped by.

"*Gahhhhhhhhhhhhhhhhhhhhhh!*" wailed Doug.

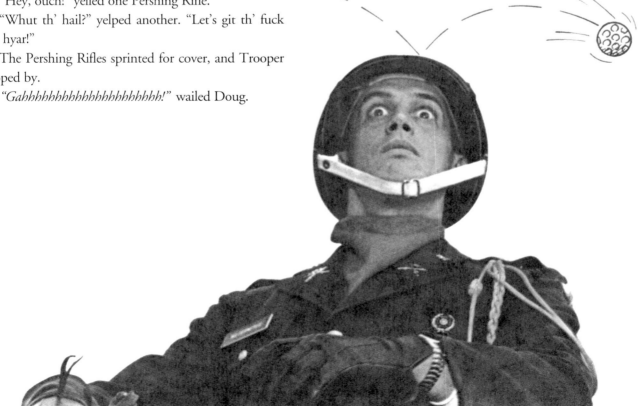

Pinto's First High

The Delta House quickly became the center of Pinto's world. He found himself spending less and less of his nights in the tiny, claustrophobic dorm room he shared with Flounder, and more and more down at the Delta bar, drinking with the brothers. At one o'clock, when Herb, the campus cop, made his nightly swing through the fraternities to see that all kegs were turned off, the Delta hard-core would repair to D-Day or Bluto's room and start on six-packs. Afterwards, Pinto would stagger back to his dorm and pass out. He'd never known life could be such fun.

On weekends there were often football games, and Boon, a superb social chairman, threw gigantic parties, ordering record-breaking quantities of half-kegs from Tanzi's, the beer store, and importing rhythm and blues combos from Philadelphia, where he had an understanding with a booking agent. Delta luminaries of the past would appear during these football weekends, such legendary personalities as Magpie, Black Whit, Troll, and Oblomov. A Delta '59 named Crazy Al arrived in the front yard in a station wagon one Saturday during pregame 'tails, opened the shotgun door, and seventeen crazed, howling dogs exploded out; Al had picked up every hound he'd seen from his home in Altoona all the way to Faber. Pinto had simply never met people like these before; he felt himself falling in love with their collective madness.

Bluto began holding pledge meetings to instruct the freshmen in booting technique, and Pinto gradually attained a certain proficiency. Flounder, however, true to his prediction, simply couldn't hack it. He gamely drank along with Bluto and the other pledges, but never once produced a boot. Bluto was patient with him, not losing faith. "Flounder, your day will come," he promised.

As the semester progressed, Pinto began to fall hopelessly behind in his work. He was still only halfway through *Paradise Lost*. He hadn't even begun his History 5 reading. He felt functionally illiterate in math and chem, and hadn't seen the inside of his French class, which met at eight A.M., since the first week of school, before the hangovers began. And now, suddenly, his one and only history paper of the semester was due Friday, and it was already Wednesday afternoon, and he hadn't even started writing. Boon found him surrounded by books on the Delta back porch, eyes glazed, hunched over a blank yellow pad.

"Whuss happ'nin'?" Boon queried.

Pinto started and looked up. "Oh, Boon. I'm in serious trouble."

"Big test?"

"No, a paper. It's due Friday and I haven't even..."

"A paper?" Boon regarded him with surprise. "You're going to *write* a paper? Why?"

"Why? Because Dean James will flunk me if I don't!"

"No, man. I mean why don't you just get a paper from Einswine? He's got the files, man."

This was the first Pinto had heard about any files. Boon hustled him up to the second floor and knocked on a door. "Swine?"

"Come," said a voice.

Einswine sat behind his desk in soiled pajama bottoms, a yellowing T-shirt, and a grubby flannel bathrobe. On his head was a green eyeshade, to cut the glare of his Tensor lamps. He was making minute, incomprehensible entries in some kind of ledger. Behind him was a bank of gray and green filing cabinets. He looked like a very smart rat in his rat's office.

"Pinto needs a history paper," Boon announced.

Einswine squinted at Pinto through his bifocals, "What century?"

"Early twentieth."

He rolled himself backward in his swivel chair to the filing cabinets. "American, Asian, or European?"

"European."

Einswine pulled open a drawer and began rummaging through it. "Long, medium, or short?"

Pinto thought. "About ten pages."

After a time, Einswine judiciously withdrew a folder and rolled himself back to the desk. "Okay. It's twelve pages on the Treaty of Brest-Litovsk, out of the University of Michigan, 1960. Used only twice and never at Faber. Guaranteed C + or better. For fifteen bucks, you retype it. For seventeen-fifty, I deliver it typed with your name on it."

"I think you better type it," Pinto decided.

"Done and done, my friend," Einswine reached out and shook Pinto's hand. "Seventeen-fifty, C.O.D. I'll see you around eleven tonight."

"Okay?" said Boon. "Now let's go meet Katy and have a beer or something."

"I hope this works," Pinto said dubiously.

"Hey!" Boon gave him a punch on the arm. "You worry too much. Let's go!"

They headed across the quad to pick up Katy after her English class. It was an incredibly crisp, perfect fall day, the trees ablaze with color, and Boon was feeling fantastic. He was still very excited about his Yankees' dramatic seventh game victory yesterday to beat the Giants in the Series; Terry, in trouble in the last of the ninth, with a one-run lead, had gotten McCovey to line out to Richardson. Boon leapt, stretching his left hand high, in imitation of Richardson's sensational, stabbing catch.

"You know how good I feel?" Boon asked Pinto. "As good as those first few moments after you get laid. You know what I mean?"

Pinto didn't answer right away. "Boon... uh, I haven't told anyone this but... actually, I've never been to bed with a woman yet."

"*What?*" Boon cried. "*You've never been laid?*"

Two passing co-eds swiveled their heads to look at Pinto, then at each other; they burst into giggles.

"Hey!" Pinto's ears flamed. He glared at Boon.

Boon laughed and leapt to spear McCovey's liner once more.

* * *

When Katy emerged from the English building, she was very excited. "Donald, listen to this: Dave Jennings invited us over to his apartment. I'm sure you can come too, Larry. Well, isn't that terrific?"

Invitations to Jennings's place were supposed to be a high-status item at Faber; Boon immediately pictured an earnest discussion of Faulkner over a china tea service.

"I'd love to go," said Larry. "I think Mr. Jennings is a *wonderful* teacher."

Swell, thought Boon sourly. He put his hands in his pockets and looked at the ground.

Katy eyed him. "You want to bring a keg along so you'll feel more at home?"

Boon laughed. "No, no, I'll intoxicate myself on his meaningful conversation." He put an arm around Katy and, with Pinto, headed in the direction of Jennings's place. "By the way, I'm trying to fix Pinto up. But it's got to be a very special girl."

Pinto felt flustered. "Boon, you don't have to..."

"She should be decent-looking, but we'll trade beauty for a certain morally casual attitude."

Katy smiled tightly. "You want someone he can fuck on the first date."

"Well put! See, Pinto's never been laid...."

"Boon! Quit it!" said Pinto.

Jennings's apartment occupied the top story of an old frame house on Oak Street. Katy led the way up the stairs. Boon looked over his shoulder at Pinto. "Hey, don't let it bother you, man. I didn't get laid until I was almost fourteen and..."

"Will you *quit it?*"

Katy stopped in front of Jennings's door and looked at Boon severely. "Don't embarrass me in front of Dave, okay? He's the only professor I like."

"I wouldn't think of it," Boon protested, all innocence.

Katy sighed and knocked.

"It's open," called Jennings's voice.

There were candles in Mateus bottles, two cats on the window sill, and many, many record albums in the brick and board bookcase; Thelonious Monk played on the hi-fi. A guitar leaned against one of the speakers and there was a sketch of Charlie Parker and a poster with a ban the bomb symbol on the wall. Jennings sat them down on cushions before a coffee table made from an old door and took a seat on the daybed sofa facing them.

Boon had never had Jennings in a class. He slowly decided, as he listened to Jennings reply to Pinto's questions about teaching, that the guy seemed pretty cool. His eyes looked a little sneaky; if he were a Delta he'd probably be called Cobra or Water Moccasin or something; definitely a snakelike quality there.

"Actually," he was saying, "teaching's just a way to pay the rent while I finish my novel."

"How long you been working on it?" Boon asked.

"Four and a half years."

"It must be very good," said Pinto, impressed.

Jennings looked pained. "It's a piece of shit." He closed his eyes and bobbed his head slightly to the music; Coltrane was soloing. All at once he asked, "You want to smoke some pot?"

"Yeah!" said Boon.

Pinto's eyes went very wide. Katy looked uncertain.

"Ever smoke before?" Jennings asked Boon.

Boon answered casually. "Sure."

Katy regarded him with skepticism. "When did you ever smoke pot?"

"I've done a lot of things you don't know about."

"Yeah," said Katy. "In the bathroom with the door locked."

Boon felt hurt. "I thought I asked you not to embarrass me in front of Dave here."

Jennings watched this exchange through halfclosed eyes. "The stuff is really special. I got it from a guy who's close friends with a black jazz musician." He went to the door, turned the key, and put the chain lock in place.

Pinto, Boon, and Katy watched his every move. Pinto was feeling highly apprehensive. Should he really do this?

Jennings pulled down the shades and laid a rolled-up towel along the base of his door, blocking the crack. With a significant glance at his audience, he went to the bookshelf, withdrew a fat Oscar Wilde – *The Complete Works* – reached into the cavity, and came out with a bulging envelope. Pinto gulped; this must be it – the stuff. Jennings crooked a finger at them and they followed him into the bathroom.

After some shuffling about, they arranged themselves in the small room: Boon and Katy face to face in the bathtub; Pinto leaning against the toilet; Jennings cross-legged on the bath mat. He lit candles and a cone of pine incense, then opened the envelope. Inside was a plastic bag. He untied the plastic bag. Inside was a packet of aluminum foil. Very slowly and carefully he opened the foil, revealing a small heap of a dried, green, herbal-looking substance and three cigarettes. The cigarettes were lumpy and uneven with their ends twisted shut.

These must be "reefers." Pinto's heart pounded. Maybe he ought to get out of here right away. Unmoving, he watched Jennings thrust an end of one of the reefers into the candle flame, lighting it. He twisted the other end open a little and brought it to his lips. With an audible sucking noise, he took in some smoke and held his breath.

Boon and Katy imitated Jennings's moves. Katy was wondering whether she'd have a mystical experience of some sort. Boon was hoping he wouldn't act like an asshole.

The joint came to Pinto. He stared at it. What if he lost control of himself? What if he immediately wanted heroin? He looked at Jennings. "I – I won't go schizo, will I?"

Jennings smiled encouragingly. "There's a distinct possibility."

Pinto brought the reefer slowly to his mouth and took a little puff. To his surprise it tasted nicer than tobacco, kind of sweet and fresh. He inhaled cautiously. "Is this right?" he asked Jennings.

"Yeah. Just, uh, try not to drool on it so much."

Pinto hazarded a more ambitious puff, drawing it deep into his lungs as he'd seen the others do. Too much! He felt the cough coming but there was nothing he could do. *Wrack hack!*

The room went dark. "Hey!" said Jennings, laughing. "You blew the candles out, man."

Pinto moderated the size of his puffs. When the first reefer was gone, Jennings lit another. Soon there were three reefer butts – Jennings called them "roaches" – lying in the ashtray. Pinto looked around. Had it happened yet? The room seemed curiously long; the door very far away. Was this it? Was he high?

All at once he noticed the music, the Monk record on automatic repeat, still playing. The way he was hearing the music was different, altered somehow. He could hear all the individual notes *and* the way they sounded together. He'd never even thought of listening to music that way before; it was great! Too bad Kent was missing out on this, he thought. Hey, Kent was a cigarette! What an amazing coincidence! They were *smoking* cigarettes, so if Kent were here then Kent would be smoking a Kent! No, wait; that wasn't right. Kent was... wait. What was he thinking about? Something to do with... he couldn't get it back. That was funny. He looked over at Boon. Boon was nuzzling Katy's neck, whispering in her ear, and she was smiling and laughing. He wished he had a girl to hold. A girl to enfold. To keep out the cold. Before he got old. Lo and be–. Pinto laughed at himself. What was his *head* doing?

Abruptly, in a blazing burst of insight, *Pinto understood the true nature of the universe.* He couldn't believe it; it had all just come to him, sitting here against the toilet. Wait'll Jennings heard *this!* He began explaining as fast as

he could; there were so many implications it took what seemed like a very long time to get to the main revelation. Jennings listened patiently.

"Okay! So that means our *whole solar system* could be like *one tiny atom* in the fingernail of some giant being."

"Mm-hm," Jennings stifled a yawn and looked attentive.

"Which means – and this is the great part – that one tiny atom in my fingernail could be..."

"A little, tiny universe?" said Jennings.

Pinto's mouth fell open. "How did you know? That's *amazing!*"

In the bathtub, Boon was serenading Katy.

Hey, hey, Paula, I want to marry you. He switched to falsetto.

Hey, Paul, I want to marry you, too.

Katy giggled and joined him for the third line.

True love mean building a life for two...

They never reached the last line.

There was silence in the bathroom as the pledge and the English prof watched them kiss, each alone with his thoughts. Then Pinto turned to Jennings.

"Could I buy some pot from you?"

There Were Giants in Those Days

"See, in the old days, the guys were *really* sick," said Hardbar. "Back when me and Bluto and Otter and D-Day were freshmen? Forget it!"

"Really?" Pinto had thought things were pretty sick right here in the present day.

"It's true," said Bluto. "You think we're sick? We're nothing. Not compared to the guys who used to be here."

A dozen Deltas stood around the basement bar on a Thursday night, drinking off a chip keg organized by D-Day earlier. James Brown was screaming from the jukebox. Hanging on the wall near the mermaid was a new sign, something produced by Hydrant in his graphics course after reading *1984*. The sign said:

SICKNESS IS HEALTH

MADNESS IS WISDOM

DRINKING IS STRENGTH

"For instance," Hardbar said, "you pledges seem to be under the impression that I'm some kind of all-time beat-off champion. Hell, my beating average is nothing compared to Crazy Al's. He was like the Babe Ruth of the genre. He wouldn't even bother to go off by himself; he'd just whip it out right here at the bar. Sometimes he used to aim at people."

D-Day shook his head, a warm, nostalgic twinkle in his eyes. "Yeah, you had to keep alert in those days. Shit, they used to have beat-off *contests* down here."

Bluto smiled hugely. "Remember those? Remember the one between Gorilla, Nosehole, and Hawk?"

The older brothers laughed. "So what happened?" Pinto asked.

Hardbar related the tale. "Gorilla was winning going away. There was no doubt about it; the boy was about to let fly any second. Then Giraffe ran up with the photograph of Gorilla's fiancée that he kept on his desk upstairs, and stuck the picture right in Gorilla's face. Gorilla's hard-on went – " Hardbar whistled a descending note. "Was Gorilla pissed! He chased Giraffe all over the house."

Otter's face was hidden behind the new *National Enquirer;* MOM BOILS BABY AND EATS HER, the headline said. "Remember that chick from Philadelphia that Tarantula used to go out with?" He put the paper down and turned to Pinto. "Tarantula was a '61. Someone fixed him up with this girl and he started dating her. He said she had zits inside her mouth."

"Gross Kay!" cried Bluto happily. "Sure. She used to hold Tarantula's cock for him while he pissed."

"The very one." Otter sighed. "You don't see many like her any more. Anyway, one night, back when I was pledging, I was up in my dorm room and there was a knock on the door. I opened it and there were Tarantula and Gross Kay, completely nude, doing a standing sixty-nine; it looked like Tarantula had a beard."

The resultant burst of laughter brought Hoover to the top of the stairs. "Ah... could you guys hold down a little? Some of us are trying to study here. Midterms start next week, you know."

"Bullshit!" Bluto roared. "Hoov, get your ass down here and drink."

"Oh, all right," Hoover trotted down the stairs and filled a glass. "What're you guys talking about?"

"The old days," said Hardbar. "Remember when Tyrannosaur got mad at the shoe store?"

"Oh, yes," said Hoover. "They sold him shoes that hurt his feet. He got drunk one night and drove a bulldozer through their front window. But he only took one pair of shoes, and he left the bad ones behind."

"Hey, where's Flounder?" Bluto asked Pinto. "He should be hearing this stuff. Maybe it'd give him some inspiration."

Pinto's mind had wandered. He was thinking about the History 5 paper he'd bought from Einswine. It had been handed back today with no marks on it, just a large *See Me* in red pencil. Pinto had arranged an appointment with Dean James for tomorrow morning, about which he was feeling a terrible sense of dread. "Kent said he'd be over later," he told Bluto. "Neidermeyer's still making him shovel out the ROTC stable every night."

D-Day tugged a large watch on a chain from one of his many zippered pockets. "He's still there at nine-thirty? *Jesus*, that Neidermeyer's an asshole."

"Hey, remember Shithouse?" Bluto addressed Pinto. "They called him Shithouse 'cause he was always drunk. One Halloween he came walking in with this pumpkin he stole from somewhere. You know, with a face carved on it and a candle inside. Well, Shithouse punched out the bottom of the pumpkin and threw the candle away. Then he tore off all his clothes and pulled the pumpkin on, like pair of shorts. The first thing you know he's got his cock hanging out the triangle that was supposed to be the pumpkin's nose, right? So he walks down the Row this way, to Omega, and knocks on the door. When they open it, there's Shithouse in the pumpkin; 'Trick or treat!' he yells. And it turns out *Dean Wormer* is inside, at an Omega invitation-only champagne dinner! Jesus, I thought they'd shit." He smiled at the memory and drained his beer. "That's the Delta *I* remember." He belched. "Christ, who does that

Neidermeyer think he is, keeping one of our pledges away from the keg all night? The Old Guys wouldn't have let this happen."

"You know, you are absolutely fucking right," said D-Day. "Let's bring the fat boy home."

The Deltas cheered and drank a round in celebration of the idea.

"Just don't get in trouble, okay?" said Hoover. "Seriously, you guys, we *are* on pro."

"Now, don't you worry your buns, Hoov," D-Day said. "We're gonna do this commando-style."

* * *

At the ROTC stable, an extremely unhappy Flounder was shoveling manure from Trooper's stall into a wheelbarrow. He would have been out of there an hour ago if the animal had just left him alone. The problem was that Trooper had come to consider Kent a playmate, and the game he liked to play was get-the-human. So far tonight, Trooper had bitten Kent five times, stepped on each of his feet at least twice, shit on his pant leg, and pissed in his socks; Kent had had to spend half his time simply avoiding injury and befoulment.

And here came the beast again; it thrust its great muzzle at Flounder, clacking its teeth an inch from the frightened boy's nose. Flounder brought the flat of his shovel up to protect his face and, on its next lunge, the horse bopped his snout on the shovel blade and recoiled, whinnying.

At that moment, Doug Neidermeyer arrived in the stall. He wore the stiff, white neck brace that had become an essential part of his wardrobe after Trooper dragged

him about the athletic field. "Dorfman! For God's sake! What kind of man hits a defenseless animal?"

Flounder was terrified. "But I... he..."

"Shut up!" Doug jabbed Flounder in the chest with a ramrod index finger, driving him against the stable wall. "I've got a good mind to smash your fat face in." He grasped Flounder's cheek between thumb and forefinger and pinched it hard. "Now listen up, you nauseating pile of blubber. Your days are numbered here at Faber, you and all your sicko Delta buddies. But, in the meantime, your ass belongs to *me*. Now drop and give me twenty!"

Flounder was acutely aware of the great quantity of horse waste still on the stall floor. "But..."

"Hit it!" Doug pushed him roughly to the ground. Flounder whimpered and began doing push-ups.

"Straight back! Your nose *will* touch the floor on each repetition! Two! Three! Four!"

As Flounder strained and grunted, Doug walked over to Trooper and stroked his nose fondly. "There now, Trooper. Good fella." The horse nuzzled him. With a secret smile, Doug took a carrot from his pocket and displayed it to Trooper. "Little treat, fella? Come and get it." Doug placed one end of the carrot in his own mouth and offered it to Trooper. The horse began nibbling on the far end, chomping closer, giving Doug a kiss as he pulled the last of it from his mouth.

Over Doug's shoulder, through a chink in the stable wall, two pairs of eyes peered, missing nothing. Flounder was still doing push-ups. Doug barked down at him, "I want these quarters standing tall by 0900 tomorrow. You

got that?" He strode off, not waiting for an answer.

Bluto and D-Day melted into the shadows at Doug's exit and waited until his footsteps had faded. Then they darted into the stable. Flounder was making pathetic attempts to clean himself with handfuls of hay. He looked on the verge of tears.

"Kent!" A sharp whisper.

Flounder looked up surprised. "Brother Bluto! Brother D-Day!" D-Day was wearing his flight suit. Bluto a black leather jacket and longshoreman's cap; both had blacked their faces with something. They looked very Guns of Navarone.

"You hate that shithead?" D-Day's breath enwreathed Flounder, beery and warm,

"Who?"

Bluto made a disgusted gesture. "Neidermeyer! You hate his guts, right?"

"I guess so," Flounder snuffled.

"You *guess* so?"

Flounder thrust his lower lip out. "Yes! Yes, I hate him. I hate his guts!"

"Good." D-Day put an arm around him. "Now, the Old Guys in Delta had a saying: 'Don't get mad; get even.'" He glanced at the horse, then began whispering in Flounder's ear. A slow smile spread across the fat pledge's face.

* * *

Moments later, Bluto, D-Day, and Flounder led the horse from the stable. It was a clear, cool night, with no moon. Bluto scouted ahead, darting from bush to tree, staying in the shadows. They reached Johnson Hall without incident, passed the statue of Emil Faber, and headed up the steps. D-Day found a key chain of lock picks in one of his zippered pockets and bent to begin fiddling at the front door.

"Watch it," cautioned Bluto. They ducked out of sight as a campus police car slowly cruised by, shining its spotlight on the pillars behind which Trooper stood. As soon as it passed, D-Day sprang back to the lock and got it open. They led Trooper inside.

Going up the marble stairs to the second floor, the clopping of the horse's hooves seemed loud as thunder in Flounder's ears. At the office entrance with the sign that read VERNON WORMER – DEAN OF STUDENTS. D-Day again knelt briefly; the door swung open. Bluto rushed across the Dean's reception room to his inner office. "Here," he called to Flounder.

Flounder took the horse inside, then reappeared alone. "Heh-heh. He's in there. Oh, boy, is this *great!*"

D-Day, stonefaced, pulled a .45 service automatic from his coat and placed it on the desk top. "Now finish it, Flounder."

Flounder's smile faded. "You're kidding."

D-Day was silent.

"I never shot anything in my life!"

Bluto was contemptuous. "I thought you hated Neidermeyer's guts."

"I do," said Flounder in a small voice.

"And what about that horse?" asked D-Day. "Is there anything in the world you hate so much as that horse?"

Flounder shook his head.

"Then get it over with, Kent," D-Day snapped the bolt on the .45 and handed it to Flounder. Flounder, zombie-like, went into the inner office.

Bluto snickered. "Just blanks, right?"

"Right."

There was a pause, then...

Bluto and D-Day rushed inside. Trooper was flat on his back, his eyes closed. Flounder stood there holding the smoking automatic.

"Holy shit!" said Bluto.

"There were *blanks* in that gun!" D-Day snatched the piece from Flounder and broke it open.

"I didn't even point the gun at him," Flounder protested frantically.

"Holy shit!" said Bluto.

"There *were* blanks in that gun," announced D-Day.

"I never hurt anything in my life," cried Flounder.

"Holy shit!" said Bluto.

The three boys looked at one another slowly.

"Yahhhhhhhhhhhhhhhhh!" Like speeded-up cartoon figures, they tore out of the building into the night. By the time they reached Delta, they were feeling quite pleased with themselves. Perhaps, Bluto thought happily, the era of the giants had not passed yet.

Bluto's Midnight Peep

The next day was to prove interesting for both the Deltas and the Omegas, but the award for "worst morning" had to go to Dean Wormer. His thoughts, when he reached his office, were on his upcoming difficult meeting with Mayor DePasto. He found his secretary with the oddest expression on her face and felt a terrible stab of foreboding.

"What's the matter?"

Miss Leonard just nodded her head in the direction of his inner office. The dean went in. A moment later he reappeared with the oddest expression on *his* face. He sat unmoving on the edge of Miss Leonard's desk while she made the call. After a time, the veterinarian showed up.

"What's the matter?"

The dean and Miss Leonard nodded their heads in the direction of the inner office. The vet went in. Who, Dean Wormer wondered suddenly, was going to break this news to Doug Neidermeyer? He just didn't think he felt up to that today. He began contriving ways to talk Miss Leonard into it.

The vet returned, repacking his instruments.

"What happened to him?" asked the Dean, genuinely curious.

"Well, I think we can rule out shooting, stabbing and poisoning. As near as I can tell, the animal died of heart failure."

"But... how did he get *in* there?" Actually, the Dean had a feeling he *knew* how the horse had gotten in there, but he asked anyway.

The vet shrugged. "And how are you going to get him out? That's the big question. He's stiff as a board!"

Idly, Dean Wormer wondered just how many other deans of America's many colleges and universities were facing this particular problem at this moment. All at once he remembered the impending arrival of the mayor. "Miss Leonard, call Buildings and Grounds. Tell them it's an emergency."

Nobody had much to say while they awaited the arrival of Mr. Michelostomy, Faber's squat, Bulgarian janitor. But when the door to the dean's office abruptly flew open, it was not Michelostomy who rushed in. It was Doug Neidermeyer.

"Dean Wormer! Someone's stolen Trooper!" Doug was badly winded, evidently having run all the way from the stables. He appeared to be in a state of shock.

"Oh, dear." Miss Leonard stood up. "I – I have to go to the powder room."

Dean Wormer shot a venomous glare after her. "Doug, I think you better sit down. You know, it's often been said

that we can judge a man by the way he..."

There was a loud knock at the door. Mr. Michelostomy stepped in, chewing the stump of a foul cigar. He carried a small, portable chain saw. "Big messy mess," he remarked agitatedly to the dean. "Yech poo!" He went into the inner office.

Doug's gaze followed him. He caught his breath sharply as he saw the four stiff white legs.

Jumping Jesus, thought the dean. Things were getting out of control here. "Doug, at times like this it takes a real man to..."

His words were lost as the chain saw roared to life. The roar changed pitch as the saw bit in. Doug's eyes rolled up and Dean Wormer moved quickly to catch him as he fainted. Someone – and he was pretty sure he knew who – was going to pay for this. But that could be attended to later. Right now he just wanted everyone, including the goddamned horse, out of here; that wop hardass would be walking in any minute.

* * *

Pinto arrived five minutes early for his appointment with kindly, white-haired Dean James, the chairman of Faber's history department. He found the man at his desk, reading student essays, puffing absently on a pipe. The dean was wearing rumpled tweeds and looked tired. Steeling himself, Pinto put on his most earnest expression.

"You wanted to see me, sir?"

James squinted up at him. "Who are you?"

God, he'd been to class so seldom the man didn't even remember him. "I'm Kroger, sir. I'm in your History 5 class, Monday, Wednesday..."

"I know when it meets, Mr. Kroger. Please sit down." Dean James consulted his History 5 grade book briefly, then looked at Pinto. "Mr. Kroger, do you know who Arnold Toynbee is?"

Pinto thought hard. "Is he that sort of fat boy who always sits in the front row?"

The dean sighed. "Arnold Toynbee is perhaps the most distinguished historian of our time. But here's the interesting part, Mr. Kroger. Your paper on Brest-Litovsk is almost identical to one that Toynbee wrote on the same subject."

Pinto felt as if a cold iron spear had just entered his gut. "Really? When did he write his?"

"Nineteen thirty-five."

"Oh, well. I wasn't even born yet."

Dean James looked pained. "Good point, Mr. Kroger. Then we know Toynbee couldn't have copied *your* work." He removed Pinto's paper from a folder on his desk and leafed through it. "You've done a remarkable job here. Quite an impressive bibliography, too. I see you've read Brunner's *Age of Conflict*. A difficult work, isn't it?"

Pinto snorted ruefully. "*Very* difficult. I'm not even sure I understood it all."

"I wouldn't be surprised. What did you think of his thesis regarding the effects of the treaty?"

"Ah... very well written." Pinto felt a tic begin on the perimeter of his left eye.

"Yes, it was." James puffed on his pipe. "I see you also read Ferguson's *Russia and the West*. Maybe you could explain to me how Ferguson's analysis of the treaty related to your paper."

"Of course." Pinto was imagining tearing off one of Boon's legs and beating Einswine to death with it. "The cause... and the effects... of the treaty can be looked at... from three major points of view." Sweat began to bead his forehead. "And those are... the social... the political, and the... economic. And the military. Did I say three points of view? I meant *four* points of..."

Dean James raised a hand. "Please, Mr. Kroger, spare me. I'd just like to know what you've been doing instead of studying."

"I'm very active in student activities."

"For instance."

"I'm... pledging a fraternity"

"Well, I hope it's worth it to you, Mr. Kroger. Because, as of now, you have a failing grade in history. I would sug-

gest that you do well on the midterm next week, or your standing at Faber could be seriously jeopardized. That's all."

* * *

The last of the horse had barely been removed from Dean Wormer's office when Mayor DePasto arrived. The dean ushered him to the armchair and at down behind his desk.

"What can I do for you, Carmine?" he asked with forced amiability.

The mayor was Sicilian, suave, and scary. He owned DePasto Oldsmobile and probably half the rest of Faber. He wasn't smiling. "Pretty soon it's your homecoming weekend. You gonna have that parade again?"

"Why, of course, Carmine. The Faber homecoming parade is the biggest event of our whole college year."

"All right, fine. You have your parade. But from now on, you wanna hold it in my town, you gotta pay."

The dean looked striken. "Carmine, I don't think it's fair for you to extort money from the college."

On "extort," the mayor's eyes glinted. "Look. Dean, as mayor of Faber I got big responsibilities. These parades are expensive. You're using my police, my sanitation people, my free Oldsmobiles. So you mention extortion again and I'll have your legs broken."

Dean Wormer sat absolutely still for a second. Some days more than other days he wished he'd run away with a circus when he was fifteen. He summoned up a friendly, conspiratorial expression. "Well, I'm sure I can arrange a nice honorarium from the student fund."

The mayor was not through. "And another thing – you better sit on that zoo fraternity of yours. I don't want no drunken riots in my town."

The dean chuckled. "Don't worry, Carmine. I've got those boys scared shitless."

For the first time since his arrival, the mayor smiled. "Good. You better hope so."

* * *

Bluto was hungry. He made his way straight through crowded, noisy Monsanto Cafeteria to the bussing window, where students were leaving their lunch trays, and began feeding off leftover salads, puddings, and french fries.

One of the great things about Faber, Bluto felt, were these free appetizers before meals.

As Bluto gobbled happily, his actions were under scrutiny by one of the wimpoid student dishwashers. The wimpoid was feeling indignant. That squat, grubby boy at the bussing window was getting away with not paying for his food! Typical of the kinds of freeloading going on in the world today, the wimpoid thought. He decided to do something about it...

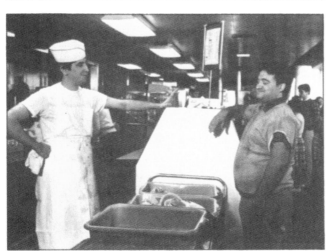
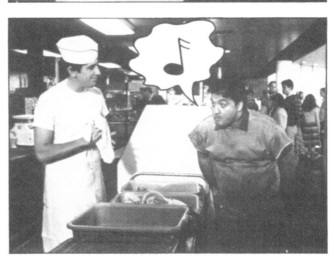

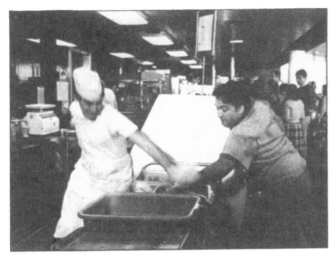

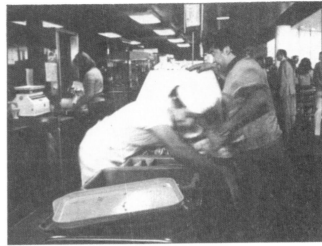

Otter, with his lunch tray, was searching for an interesting spot to sit. He saw Mandy Peppridge, alone at one of the window tables. The otter's smile came over his face and he walked over to her.

"Mandy! Why, I haven't seen you since last spring. You know, the night we..."

"Go away." Mandy was all ice. She wore a cashmere sweater with a circle pin and her long blond hair was back in a stylish flip. She looked, as always, gorgeous.

"Sorry, but I can only stay a minute." Otter sat down next to her. "Can I buy you some lunch? Oh, I see you've already got some lunch. How 'bout some milk, then? Oh, you've got milk, too." He turned the grin on her; a thousand irresistible smile lines radiated outward from his eyes. "Well, then, can I massage your white thighs while you eat?"

Mandy was unamused. "Do *I* have to leave?"

"No Mandy, is that any way to treat an *intimate* friend?"

"I was drunk that night." She looked defensive.

"Mmm. On three whole cups of punch, I seem to recall."

Over Otter's shoulder Mandy could see Gregg, Babs, and Chip Diller leaving the cafeteria line, heading over to join her. She began to feel panicky.

"I asked you never to speak to me again! Now will you *go away?*"

*   *   *

At the Pershing Rifles' table, Doug Neidermeyer sat unmoving before his meal. Several of the Rifles were with him, eating with straight backs and great efficiency, but none dared speak to the commander, so great was his grief. All around them, Monsanto Cafeteria was filled with the clamor of conversation; at their table, a terrible silence reigned.

Abruptly, directly behind Doug, there was a loud whinny. The Rifles looked up in horror. Bluto was walking by with a hugely-laden tray; he whinnied again and blew air through his lips. Doug spun in fury, causing a bolt of pain in his neck. *"Arrrrrhhhh!"* he cried, grimacing. Bluto, whistling the "William Tell Overture," continued on his way.

*   *   *

Otter answered Mandy's request with another smile, making no move to leave. He was enjoying her discomfiture enormously. Gregg, Babs, and Chip arrived at the table and sat down opposite them, Gregg eyeing Otter suspiciously. "Hello, Stratton," he said coolly. "Congratulations on your rush week."

"Hello, Gregg," Otter replied pleasantly. "Congratulations on your haircut."

"Wise-ass," said Chip.

"I hope we're not interrupting anything, Mandy, honey," Babs said coyly.

"Well, if you must know..." Otter began.

"Eric was just leaving," said Mandy.

Otter looked at her innocently. "No, I wasn't."

Gregg's neck was getting red. "I could *make* you leave if you..."

A loud clatter of dishes cut Gregg off. Bluto was sitting down with them. His tray contained a small mountain of assorted edibles.

Otter was delighted. "Bluto! Hi! I think you know everyone here."

For a tense, unblinking moment, Bluto stared straight at Mandy. Then he began to feed. The topmost item on his tray was a plate of mashed potatoes with gravy. Bluto attacked it with zeal, jamming impossibly large forkfuls of the stuff into his mouth so that perhaps a third of each bite fell back onto his plate.

Mandy recoiled. "Really, Gregg, can't you..."

"Don't worry," said Otter. "Just keep your hands and feet away from his face."

Bluto laughed appreciatively; several more gobbets of potato fell from his mouth.

Babs was revolted. "This is absolutely gross. That boy is a pig."

Bluto stiffened, but continued to eat.

"Yeah," put in Chip, "I can smell him from here."

Bluto's eyebrows twitched ominously; he swallowed and poured a carton of milk down his throat.

Gregg shook his head in angry disbelief. "Don't you have any respect for yourself?"

Bluto's nostrils flared; he looked up at Gregg, Babs, and Chip. "See if you can guess what I am now." He jammed five more quick forkfuls of mashed potato into

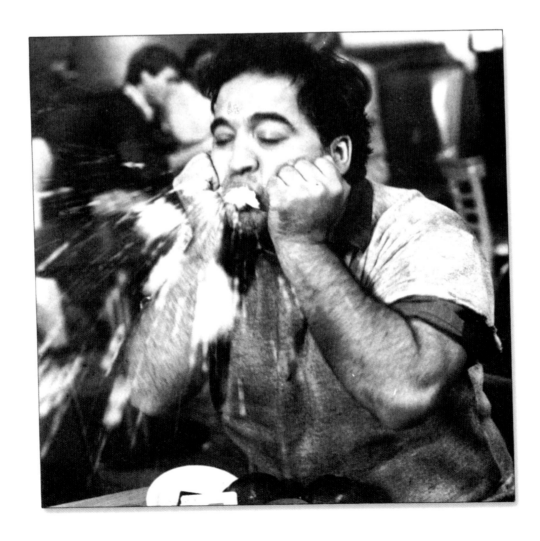

his mouth so that his cheeks bulged alarmingly, then slammed his fists hard against both sides of his face. Heavily-gravied mashed potatoes fired from his mouth with great velocity to splatter the horrified Gregg, Babs, and Chip.

"I'm a zit. Get it?" said Bluto brightly.

Otter laughed with delight. Gregg snarled like an animal. He grabbed a handful of Bluto's sweatshirt. "All right, you bastard! Right here! Let's go!"

Bluto waggled his eyebrows in mock terror, broke away from Gregg easily, and zipped down a row of tables. Gregg and Chip took off in hot pursuit.

Making a big turn at the end of an aisle, Bluto collided with a passing student and sent his tray flying. The tray landed dead center on the Pershing Rifles' table. Milk, gravy, Jell-O, and bits of salad flew in all directions, defiling the Rifles' immaculate uniforms.

"That's it!" said Doug Neidermeyer. *"Charge!"*

The Rifles rushed from the table to join the chase. Most of the other students in the cafeteria were on their feet now, following the action with great interest. A few of them started a familiar chant: "Food fight, food fight, food fight, food fight...." In the kitchen, the cooks and servers exchanged nervous glances.

Bluto dodged the outstretched arms of Chip Diller and sped down another aisle, a whole line of Omegas and Pershing Rifles trailing him. "I'll kill you, Blutarski!" Gregg shrieked. "I'll physically kill you!"

More students were chanting. "Food fight! Food fight! Food fight!"

Otter and Mandy were now alone.

"Why don't we go out tonight, Mandy?"

She turned from the growing chaos in the cafeteria to gaze at him. "Don't flatter yourself, Otter. It wasn't that great." She gathered up her books, stood, and walked away with a toss of her hips.

"Not great?" said Otter to himself, incredulously.

Doug Neidermeyer's pursuit capability was limited, due to his bad neck, so he'd been standing in the center of the cafeteria, howling orders. Now he saw his own personal chance; Blutarski was running straight at him. With the neck brace, Doug looked not unlike the Frankenstein monster as he lurched forward, arms spread wide, to grab the enemy. Bluto was too quick for him; he ducked under Doug's closing arms and the entire mob chasing him crashed into the ROTC commander, smashing him flat.

"Aiiiiieeeee!" Doug screamed.

"Food fight! Food fight! Food fight!"

Bluto inspected the heap of Omegas and Pershing Rifles with satisfaction. A freshman was passing with his lunch tray, and Bluto hurled him on top for good measure, adroitly plucking the boy's wedge of chocolate cake from his tray as he went down. He winged the cake across the room and roared...

FOOD FIGHT!

The cafeteria erupted like a sudden fireworks display. Rolls flew, hamburgers sailed, salads broke up and dispersed. Puddings made great splatting impact sounds as they landed. Apples and ice cream whizzed by. Single plates of spaghetti covered incredible radii.

Cafeteria workers cowered behind the steam tables. Co-eds screamed and ran for the exits. Bluto ducked out a back door just as the campus cops were coming in the front. Whistling happily, he headed for town. Lunch had been great, but he hadn't had a chance to finish; he wanted to make a stop at Pop's Pizza before his two o'clock class.

* * *

The pledgemaster was in such a good mood that he called a booting practice for that evening. Pinto threw several good power boots and won Bluto's special esteem; booting had become rather easy and fun for him by now, a friendly, good-natured way of showing off his Delta prowess to the brothers. Flounder, as usual, had no luck and had to be helped to the tube room to sleep it off.

Katy prevailed upon Boon to take her to the new Ingmar Bergman film, which he glumly agreed to do. Ot-

ter prevailed upon his date to meet him an hour early and drove her out to the Rainbow Motel in his red Corvette, feeling delighted to be alive. D-Day, with a paperback *Hamlet* in a pocket of his flight suit, made it out to Echo Lake on his bike and recited sonorous soliloquies into the dusk, getting chills at some of the passages.

Stork, poised before the second-floor bathroom mirror, was practicing his draw. He'd recently welded a metal hook to the protruding end of his slide rule; by now he could whip it out of the holster, give it a double spin, and have it flat in both hands, ready to compute. "Twenty-seven pi over the cube of fifty-nine!" he honked at his reflection. The slide rule flashed in his hands. "Twenty-three point six six six!" He clicked his stopwatch; four point eight seconds. Stork allowed himself a burst of pride. He was getting *good*.

Hardbar strolled downtown to Fletcher's, where he purchased the latest issues of *Playboy, Topper, Rogue,* and *Gent*. He went back to the house, tapped himself a couple of pitchers, and retired to his room for several hours. Mountain, Hydrant, and Snot went on a road trip to Emily

Dickinson; they'd just given up all hope of getting dates and were headed for the City Café, a local truckers' bar, for some boilermakers. Hoover, worried about midterms, was sneak-booking at the libes.

Doug Neidermeyer was in his room at Omega House, hanging up his uniform. He'd just come from disciplining some freshman cadets, really scaring them badly, and his mood was much improved over its earlier state, after that painful, humiliating scene in the cafeteria. He stood before his dresser in socks, garters, and shorts, and tried a smile on himself in the mirror. "Hi, there. Doug Neidermeyer." He made the smile slightly smaller and modified his stance. "Doug Neidermeyer. Nice to see you." Satisfied, he turned his attention to the battle layout on his dresser top. *"Vrummmmm vrummmmm,"* he rumbled, pushing forward a small, plastic tank, advancing it on several toy soldiers pinned down behind his cuff link box. One of the soldiers had a tiny bazooka; Doug brought him to his feet. *"Vrooooshhhhh!"* he said. *"P-kow!"* He toppled the tank over onto its back, laughing out loud.

At nine o'clock, Otter returned from the Rainbow and dropped his date at her sorority. She was petulant.

"But it's so early, Eric."

"Sorry, Kathy. My molecular bonding paper's due Friday."

She made a face, but Otter gave her a kiss and she smiled.

"I love you, Eric."

Otter hugged her. "I do, too."

She got out of the Corvette and skipped up the walk. Otter waved fondly and pulled away from the curb.

Gregg Marmalard and Mandy Peppridge, in Gregg's white MG, were parked at Pencil Point, overlooking the twinkling lights of Faber. A few other cars were parked at discreet distances.

"It's certainly a beautiful night." Mandy was giving Gregg a hand job; both stared straight ahead.

"Mmm," said Gregg. "Little overcast, though. No stars."

"Oh, look, there's a star. Let's make a wish. Star light, star bright..."

"That's not a star. It's moving too fast."

"Oh."

"Too small for a 707," Gregg mused. "Must be a twin Beechcraft or something."

Mandy felt the familiar sense of great boredom, like a lead cloak, begin to descend on her. Up and down moved her hand.

"Probably leased," Gregg went on. "It's getting harder and harder to write off the overhead on those babies."

"Gregg, do you think you'll be finished soon? My arm's getting tired."

"Sorry, Mandy. I guess I'm a little distracted because of that business with the Deltas today." He glanced at her. "God knows how many different women they try to molest."

Mandy switched hands. "Anything happening yet?"

"Maybe a little slower." He paused. "I guess some women are reluctant to report these things." He glanced at her again.

"How's this?"

"Yes, that's good." Gregg swallowed. "I bet that Eric Stratton's lucky he's not in *jail*."

Up and down, up and down. "I'll say."

Gregg tensed. "What?"

"Hmmmm?"

"You'll say what?"

"I'll say what?"

Gregg shook his head with exasperation. "No, *you* said, 'I'll say' when *I* said Eric Stratton should be..."

"Gregg, my arm is really starting to hurt. Darn it, if you're not even going to try, I'm going to *stop*." She pulled away from Gregg and, with loud snapping sounds, peeled the two surgical rubber gloves from her hands.

In his room at Delta, Hardbar inspected with interest a page featuring women in black underwear and garter belts. One of the great things about beating yourself off, he reflected, was that you could do it so much *better* than any of the girls could.

By nine-thirty, Otter was back in the parking lot at the Rainbow Motel, this time with Doris Deitz, a blond

English major with an adorable ass. Otter leapt out of the Corvette, doctor's bag in hand, and opened Doris's door. She pouted up at him.

"I'm still mad," she said. "I waited two hours."

Otter loved her when she pouted; she had great lips for it. "I *am* sorry. Sometimes I get so absorbed in my studies I forget all about the time."

Doris got out of the car and took his arm. "You're such a bullshitter," she whispered, giving his ear a kiss, and pulled him toward the room.

There was a keg lapse at Delta, and Bluto set out for town to get a few interim six-packs. He walked along Sorority Row, tunelessly grunting "He's a Rebel," feeling at peace with all things. Abruptly, Gregg Marmalard's MG drove by him and pulled to a halt in front of the Tri Pi house. *Mandy,* thought Bluto. He hurled himself behind some bushes.

Mandy got out and Gregg followed her up the walk. At the door she gave him a quick, prim kiss and went inside. Gregg thrust his hands in his pockets and walked rapidly back to the car. The minute he pulled away, Bluto emerged from the bushes and crawled rapidly into the pool

of shadow thrown by the great oak tree that stood beside the house.

Mountain, Hydrant, and Snot, fortified with a case of Carlings, had reluctantly begun the milk run back to Faber in Snot's '54 Ford. Stork had holstered his slide rule and Hardbar had stored his magazines under the bed; Hoover was back from the libes. Boon had returned unsmiling from Katy's a little earlier and instantly bought a house keg, solving the lapse problem. Now he hung out morosely by the jukebox, playing tormented R&B love ballads, refusing to let anyone else pick a song. Hardbar challenged Stork to a pinball series on the Williams "Three Deuces" and beat him four games out of seven.

Otter got Doris back to her dorm around midnight. They norgled in a shadowy corner of the lobby until the grad student behind the sign-in desk cleared her throat pointedly. By degrees, Doris pulled away.

"I love you, Otter."

"Me, too."

She tilted her face up for one last kiss and ran to the desk.

"You'll have to leave now. I'm locking up."

Otter opened his eyes. The grad student was standing impatiently over him. She had a pixie cut, green eyes, and sensational legs. Otter sighed, stood up, and began trudging wearily toward the door. Then he stopped and turned back to her.

"What time are you finished here?"

* * *

Bluto sat with his back against the oak tree, uncertain about what to do next. A flicker of movement at the periphery of his vision made him look up. Mandy was passing a window a few feet over his head, on her way upstairs. He scrambled to his feet, just in time to get a quick glance up her skirt as she disappeared from view. Too soon! He wanted more! He tried jumping up and down; it didn't help. He looked about in frustration, and his eyes fell on the oak. Like some dawn-era, tree-dwelling anthropoid, he scurried up the trunk.

By the time he'd climbed about twenty feet he was grunting with exertion. He crawled out onto a limb, parted the leaves in front of him... and found himself in paradise. He was directly in front of a bedroom window, and there were about seven or eight Tri Pis in there – in bras and panties and stockings and garter belts! In fact, some of them had their tits out! He was seeing the *nipples* of girls he'd sat next to in class! *And there was some bush!!* "Uhhhhh..." said Bluto. He didn't know where to look first!

There was a flash of movement to his left. Mandy was at the window of the next room! She was down to her underwear!! Oh, God, thought Bluto, I'd like to juice *her* keisters. He crawled further out on the limb, closer to her room, and pushed the leaves aside.

Her bra was gone and... *she was fondling her own breasts!* Mandy Peppridge, gazing dreamily into the night not ten feet away from him, was holding and snuggling and tracing her fingernails over her very own juicy, wonderful set of beefsteak tomatoes! *"Fuhhhhhhhhh..."* said Bluto.

Then Mandy slid a hand slowly down over the slim firmness of her tummy, into her panties, affording Bluto a brief glimpse of her downy, golden nether hair. Biting her lip, she began to move the hand, slowly and teasingly at first, then with greater speed. Bluto's jaw was resting on the tree limb; he had to get closer. He began edging forward again.

The limb snapped.

"Yahhhhhhhhhh..." said Bluto.

Thud!

"You're ten minutes late, Doris," the grad student told her. "That gives you twenty late-minutes altogether. Better watch it."

Doris hardly heard her. She waved at Otter, threw him a kiss, and went upstairs. Otter sank into a lounge chair and closed his eyes. He felt exhausted. Maybe he was getting old; why, when he'd been a sophomore he'd been able to...

Midterms

Midterm exam week hit Faber like an epidemic of flu, stopping all social activity cold. Ironically, it was during this period of void that Doug Neidermeyer finally got something on the Deltas.

When Gregg had originally given Doug the assignment of finding a way to revoke Delta's charter back in September, Doug had accepted with pleasure and immediately attacked the problem enthusiastically, forming the Omega pledges into a reconnaissance platoon and keeping the Delta House under constant, covert surveillance. Thus far, other than a few late-night sightings of Deltas urinating in their front yard, nothing substantive had turned up. To really nail the lid on the Delta coffin, Doug needed something big, nasty, and undeniable. He waited patiently.

It was Chip Diller who finally brought in the crucial bit of intelligence, which he had picked up while monitoring a conversation between Blutarski and Day through a knothole in the rear wall of the Delta garage: five Delta seniors were taking Psychology 101. The midterm fell on Thursday, and Day and Blutarski were planning a nightly search through the psychology building trash to find the discarded test stencil.

Doug thought for a moment, then smacked his fist into his palm. "We've got 'em! Now, listen up, Chip; here's what I want you to do."

Down the Row, blithely unaware of the disciplinary mine fields that lay ahead, the Deltas got down to studying. Bluto prepared for his comp lit exam by reading several Classic Comics. Flounder hid in the library, memorizing his French vocabulary cards. Stork was taking all engineering courses, which he always aced without booking, so he continued work on his plans for a new Delta tap system that would provide a spigot in every room of the house, including the bathrooms. Otter contrived to get laid by some of the smarter girls in his classes and poured over their notes. Boon studied down in the bar, by the jukebox. He'd always, since early high school, done his academic work listening to rock 'n' roll; in addition, this study area placed him mere steps from the keg. And Hardbar was booking in the art library where, when fatigued with his reading, he could sneak back into the stacks and slam the ham to nudes by Titian and Rubens.

Pinto was in a total panic. The only course that didn't worry him was English, since Mr. Jennings didn't believe in marks and always passed everyone. But he was up shit creek as far as the rest of his courses were concerned. His only chance was some truly in-

credible cramming. When Einswine set a cannister of small pills-labeled STUDY AIDS – 5¢ on the table by the Delta stairs, Pinto purchased several, locked himself in his room, and opened his first book.

Hoover was doing *his* studying in his room at Delta. There was a basketball hoop affixed to the wall across from the sofa, hung with brassieres instead of netting; Hoover was balling up his class notes, page by page, and shooting baskets.

D-Day stuck his head in. "Bookin', Hoov?"

"Mm-hm." He bounced one off the rim.

"Can I join ya?"

"Mm-hm."

D-Day sat down with Hoover, opened his looseleaf, and began balling up his own notes. By the end of exam week, Hoover had eked out a narrow victory, 1,006 to 998.

* * *

Chip, acting on reliable intelligence from Terry Auerback, an honors psych major, was able to hit the mimeograph room immediately after the test was run off. He pulled the wet, sticky blue stencil from the wastebasket and replaced it with another wet, sticky blue stencil, this one prepared by him, Terry, and Doug Neidermeyer at Omega House. As Chip slipped from the room, Mr. Michelostomy came in the rear door, pulling a trash barrel on a wheeled stand. The disgusting old guy drew a pint of Thunderbird from his jacket and had a few swallows. Smacking his lips, he put the bottle away, emptied the wastebasket into his trash barrel, and continued his rounds.

* * *

That night, in their commando gear, Bluto and D-Day made a daring raid on the dumpster behind the psychology building. After much rooting about, Bluto came up with a sticky, crumpled blue stencil. D-Day wielded his pencil flash: "Psychology 101 Midterm Examination" the stencil said. They smiled broadly, slapped palms, and stole off into the darkness.

Only then did Doug and Chip step from the shadows at the far end of the building. They exchanged shit-eating grins and trotted toward the Row to report to Gregg.

* * *

On Wednesday, Boon went to Einswine with the test stencil and asked him to determine the correct answers to the fifty multiple-choice questions. Einswine suggested brightly that he ought to be paid plenty for, in effect, taking an entire extra midterm. Boon reminded Einswine of his failure to pay any social dues the last three semesters running and of the vast quantities of brew he'd consumed nonetheless. Grumbling, Einswine reached for the stencil. An hour later, he brought a list of the answers to Otter, Boon, Bluto, D-Day, and Hoover, who were down with the keg. He was heartily toasted, and the boys set to writing their own copies of the list on tiny pieces of notebook paper.

* * *

At eleven o'clock, Pinto decided he'd better pull another all-nighter. His eyes hurt and he was grinding his teeth incessantly. Maybe another pill would help. He dropped his last remaining benny and turned back to his books.

* * *

The following morning, Bluto, D-Day, Otter, Boon, and Hoover strolled into the Psych 101 room just as the student proctors were handing out the test papers. They found seats and began quickly filling out their answer sheets.

In the History 5 classroom, Pinto's pill power was rapidly running out. The faster everyone around him wrote, the slower his pencil moved. He could hardly read the questions. Presently, he slumped forward, his eyes closing. He'd just rest for a minute. Soon he was dreaming that he was thirty-seven years old and still hadn't graduated or gotten laid.

* * *

On Friday at five, the last midterms ended. The living room at Delta was crowded with drinking brothers.

"So how'd it go, Boon?" Hardbar called from the card table. "You guys ace the psych test?"

"Looks like it, thanks to the dorkbreath twins here." Boon waved a hand at Bluto and D-Day, sitting next to him on the sofa. The dorkbreath twins waggled their eyebrows roguishly, clinked their brimming beer mugs together, and drank deeply.

Otter was on the hall phone, a finger in one ear to keep out the clamor. "Your mother died? Oh, I'm sorry to hear that." He listened for a moment. "Well, do you think breaking our date is going to bring her back to life? Don't you think she'd want you to go out and have a good time?"

Boon went over to sit with Pinto, who was sprawled miserably on the chair beneath the moose head.

"You look terrible."

"I feel terrible. I think I flunked everything." Pinto's eyes were extremely bloodshot and he felt as if rats were gnawing on his spine.

Otter walked over and sat down with them. "She broke our date," he told Boon.

"Washing her hair?"

"Dead mother."

Hoover entered the room with a look of alarm on his face and rushed straight to Boon and Otter.

"We're in trouble. I just checked with the guys over at the Jewish house and every one of our answers on the psych test was wrong."

Boon was incredulous. *"Every one?"* He glared at Bluto and D-Day. "Those assholes must have stolen the wrong exam! Either that or Einswine's cruisin' for an incredible…"

"Oh, God," whispered Otter. "Look what just creeped in."

The Deltas' eyes widened in horror; twenty-two hands hid twenty-two beers in a flash of sudden, simultaneous movement. Dean Wormer stood in the front hall. He took in the paint-splattered walls, the naked female window dummy with the Brillo pad pasted to its groin, the basic sense of grunge that was the Delta ambience; his face registered revulsion. He walked to the entrance of the living room.

"Well, well, well. It looks like somebody forgot that there's a rule against alcoholic beverages in fraternities on probation."

"What a tool," muttered Otter, disgusted.

"I didn't catch that, son," the dean snapped. "What did you say?"

Otter stood, the picture of innocence. "I said, what a *shame* it is that a few bad apples can spoil everybody's good time by breaking the rules. I think the bad apples know who they are."

The dean's eyes narrowed. "Put a sock on it, son, or you'll be out of here like shit through a goose." Otter quickly sat back down. "Have you boys seen your house grade point average?" He looked from Delta to Delta. "Well, have you?"

Reluctantly, Hoover stood up. "I have, sir. I know it's a little below par at the moment."

"It's more than a little below par, Mr. Hoover. It stinks! It's the lowest on campus. It's the lowest in Faber history."

"Well, sir," Hoover ventured, "we're hoping that our midterm grades will really help our average."

Boon burst out laughing. He couldn't help it.

Dean Wormer swiveled his head to regard Boon balefully. "Laugh now. You clowns have been on double secret probation since the beginning of this semester."

Otter looked at D-Day. "Double secret probation?"

D-Day shrugged.

"That means one more slip-up, one more mistake, and this fraternity has had it at Faber!" Nailing them with a last awful look, the dean turned and made his way from the house.

The Deltas were silent a long moment.

"Well!" said Boon at last. "'That was pleasant. Nice of him to stop by, don't you think?"

Hoover was very upset. "We gotta do something. He's serious this time. He must know about the exams."

"You're right, Hoov," said Otter. "This *is* serious."

Boon nodded. "We gotta do something." He looked at Otter. "Toga party?"

Otter smiled.

"Otter!" Hoover was beside himself. "We're on double secret probation, whatever that is. We can't..."

"Hey!" shouted Boon to the room. "You guys up for a toga party?"

"Hail, yes!" chirped Stork. "Yah-hah!"

"To-ga!" Bluto lumbered to his feet and began a strange, lurching dance. "To-ga to-ga to-ga!"

A few at a time, the other brothers took up the chant. *"To-ga to-ga to-ga!"* They began to imitate the dance moves of Bluto, and soon all the Deltas were jumping up and down like huge, demented children.

"I think they like the idea," Otter observed.

Hoover shook his head helplessly. "Otter, Boon, please don't do this."

"I got news for you, Hoov," said Otter. "They're gonna get us no matter what we do, so we might as well have a good time."

Hoover sighed. He looked at the guys careening happily around the room. Oh, well, what the hell?

He began jumping up and down, too. *"To-ga to-ga to-ga!"*

Boon found Katy that evening at the Laundromat, removing a pile of their mutual laundry from the dryer. He began helping her fold clothes, shifting his gooey piece of pizza from hand to hand as required. When he broke the news about the party, her reaction was not what he'd been hoping for.

"No-thank-you, Boon. I'm not in the mood for an orgy."

"It's not going to be an orgy. It's a *toga* party" Absently, he sniffed a pair of her panties. She snatched them away.

"Honestly, Boon. You're twenty-one years old. In six months you'll be a college graduate and tomorrow night you're going to wrap yourself up in a sheet and pour beer over your head. It's really cute, but I think I'll pass this time."

Boon was nonplussed. "You want me to go alone?"

She touched his hand. "Baby, I don't want you to go at all."

"But it's a fraternity party. And I'm in the fraternity. How can I miss it?"

"I'll write you a note. I'll say you're too well to attend."

Boon drew up angrily. "Funny. Very fucking funny." He spun and walked out, slamming the door behind him.

"I love you," Katy called softly. Sighing, she pulled a pair of Boon's shorts, ratty and full of holes, from the laundry pile. "Gross," she said, folding them.

Toga Party

The following day, the Deltas were up and moving before noon, preparing for the party. Boon assigned the job of making the supply run to himself and Otter, but when they walked out the front door of the house on their way to the supermarket, the vision that awaited them in the front yard stopped them dead in their tracks. Flounder was there, with a gleaming new 1963 Lincoln Continental! Pinto, on the front steps, was watching him polish it lovingly with a soft chamois cloth.

"Holy shit," breathed Boon. "Where'd he get the wheels?"

Pinto looked up. "From his brother. He's letting him use it for a couple of weeks. Kent invited his girlfriend up for the weekend."

D-Day roared into the yard on his Harley, whipped off his goggles, and stared at the Lincoln with unabashed desire. Almost reverently, he opened the hood to inspect the engine. Flounder polished away, a proud smile filling the lower half of his great round face.

Otter came off the steps and threw an affable arm around Kent. "Flounder, I'm making you pledge representative to the social committee."

"Hey, thanks, Otter!" A suspicious look replaced his smile. "What do I have to do?"

"You have to drive us to the Food King!"

Otter hustled Flounder into the driver's seat while Boon and Pinto jumped in from the other side. D-Day slammed the hood and the big car pulled from the yard.

The supermarket was almost empty, which fit Boon's plans nicely. He grabbed a shopping cart, and with Pinto in tow, walked down an aisle, idly throwing a few bags of pretzels and potato chips into the cart. When they reached the meat department, Boon stopped.

"Pinto, unzip that sweater a bit. About halfway down... right." He took a large sirloin steak from the meat cooler and, with a quick glance in either direction, slipped it into Pinto's sweater. "Just keep it closed and follow me."

Pinto was too surprised to say a word. Boon snatched up a second steak, then pretended to study it elaborately as a lady shopper in a fur coat walked by, pushing her cart. As soon as she was out of sight, he stuffed the second steak in with the first.

"Hey!" Pinto laughed. "I could get in trouble."

"That's right. So be cool."

* * *

Flounder had started out following Otter, but when the senior casually threw a bottle of Mazola oil high in the air over his shoulder, which Kent just barely caught, he decided to look around on his own. He stood now before the candy display. He hadn't realized it, but you could buy entire boxes of Milky Way bars and huge, oversized bags of M&Ms here. If there was going to be some sort of a big party at the house tonight, as he had just been told, the brothers would certainly want to have some candy around. Sissy, his girl, was very fond of Chocolate Babies; he took a couple of bags from the shelf and hefted them, trying to

see which was heavier. Suddenly, perversely, one of the bags slipped from his grasp, fell and burst. A number of Chocolate Babies spun out, little brown whirls on the shiny supermarket floor. *Oops*, thought Flounder. He quickly replaced the bag on the shelf, turning it so that the rip didn't show, and began eating the evidence.

* * *

Otter, meanwhile, had wandered to the men's toiletries display. He was wondering whether to buy some Canoe, the new aftershave that was currently being heavily advertised on the tube, but when he sniffed it he found it much too sweet. He snickered; Gregg Marmalard would probably wear stuff like that on his dates with Mandy. Otter guessed he would remain an Old Spice man a while longer.

The woman in the fur coat walked by and Otter followed her with his eyes to the produce department. To his surprise, she reached into her purse, withdrew a pocket flask, and knocked back a good-sized belt from it. Otter smiled; the woman wasn't bad-looking. A bit matronly, perhaps, but still well within his range of acceptability. The fur coat was hanging open and he could make out a pretty good set in there. Cheerfully, he headed toward her.

She was inspecting a cucumber, so Otter took one, too. She looked up and he smiled at her. "Mine's bigger than that."

"I beg your pardon!"

"My cucumber. It's bigger."

The woman laughed and looked him over. Otter's infallible inner detection mechanism registered lust readings; his smile widened. "Vegetables can be really sensuous, don't you think?"

"No," she corrected him. "Vegetables are sensual. *People* are sensuous."

"Right! Sensual. That's what I meant. By the way, my name's Eric Stratton. They call me Otter."

"My name's Marion. They call me Mrs. Wormer."

He blinked. "How interesting. We have a *Dean* Wormer at Faber."

"What a coincidence," Marion said drily. "I have a husband called Dean Wormer at Faber."

Otter's mouth fell open.

Marion laughed and took a swig from her flask. "Still want to show me your cucumber?"

* * *

When they got to the check-out counter, Boon handed Pinto five dollars. "Take care of this, will you?" With a wave at the shopping cart of potato chips and pretzels, he walked out of the store. Pinto gulped. The front of his sweater bulged as if he had unborn quadruplets in there.

"I think you gained a little weight since you came in," observed the check-out girl.

To Pinto's surprise he found himself looking at the pretty blond teenager he'd met at Pop's Pizza after the first night of rushing. And now she would almost certainly turn him in, probably getting him thrown out of school. He looked at her beseechingly. "It's just a prank. I'm pledging a fraternity."

She popped her gum and gave him a sunny smile. "Don't sweat it, sweetie. I won't tell." She began ringing up the visible stuff in his cart.

Pinto beamed at her.

* * *

"I'm old enough to be your mother," Marion said to Otter. "Besides, I have to go to the goddamn Senior Honors Banquet tonight."

Otter shrugged genially. "Well, maybe some other time."

"Doubtful," said Marion, but with a little smile.

Otter skipped off toward the check-out lines. He found Flounder at the candy section. "Kent! We're out of here."

According to her supermarket name tag, the girl's name was Clorette. "So, if you're not busy, would you like to go to a fraternity party?" Pinto asked her.

"Will I be home by twelve?"

"Sure! Anytime you want. I'll pick you up at..."

Clorette cut him off. "Better not. My dad would kill me if he knew I was going to a fraternity house. He *hates* them. How 'bout I meet you there? Is that okay?"

"Is it okay?" Pinto gazed at her pretty smile and ripe young breasts. "It's terrific!"

* * *

The afternoon passed in a flurry of activity at Delta House. The phone was constantly busy as the brothers lined up dates. Stork called Flamingo, his engineering department quasi-girl friend. D-Day, Hoover, and Mountain got dates. Even Hardbar got a date... with Mary Lee Kelly, the hand job specialist. And, of course, Boon alerted the Delta girls, that loose group of Faber co-eds who actually enjoyed partying at Delta. Some were gorgeous, others were beasts; the common factor was that all of them could really hurl down beers and throw horror shows with the brothers, and that short of biting a chicken's head off before their eyes, you couldn't gross them out. The Delta girls were a breed apart.

The truck from Tanzi's backed up to the Delta front porch and began unloading half-kegs. Boon hooked one of them up for the early drinkers, then dipped into the social fund to pay for them. Noting that there was barely enough left to pay for the band, he went to the phone and called Walton Liquors.

"We'll pick it up in about an hour. That's a case of vodka, six quarts of grain alcohol, and two cases of grape juice. Right. Mar-ma-lard. Gregg Marmalard. And you can just put it on the Omega account."

Bluto supervised decorations, which consisted of toilet paper looped about the basement like bunting and two dozen rubbers blown up and hung from the ceiling beams. Dumptruck and Snot placed in every bathroom a cardboard carton with a slot cut in the top, scrawling in black crayon on each, "Put 'em here, girls!" Other brothers sat around constructing bed-sheet togas, exchanging beady-eyed looks of anticipation. Toga parties were noted for their high make-out potential. With all that flesh on view, and with the Purple Jesus punch Boon and Mountain were currently blending in a washtub with their feet, things would get very steamy around midnight.

At seven, a battered station wagon pulled into the Delta front yard. It was royal blue, had mud flaps, and bore on its side the legend OTIS DAY & THE KNIGHTS. Boon rushed to the door and watched in near-ecstasy as the station wagon poured out Negroes. Cool city black guys were rare as chocolate egg creams in Faber, Pennsylvania. Two of them were wearing do-rags! Greatly excited, he rushed down to meet them. His first move would be to get them down to the bar where they could hear the jukebox and become aware of Delta's hipness level. The typical fraternity at Faber listened to white rock 'n' roll bands playing Duane Eddy-type material, and Boon wanted Otis Day to get, right off, that here at Delta he could play any funky Negro thing he wanted, that he shouldn't feel as if he were performing for a "white audience."

Hardbar directed the shifting of the pinball games to the furnace room. Boon's old high school buddy, Amherst Frog, showed up with two Chinese dates and a bottle of J&B. Mountain set out the punch. The Knights were setting up at the far end of the room; tentative electric guitar sounds and drum rim shots could be heard. Gradually, the brothers began to appear in their Roman garb. Otter's toga fit as if it had been tailored for him; perhaps, amidst the enormous stores of his wardrobe, he had always had a toga, waiting for its moment to come. Boon wore his best pair of shades and an orange letter sweater over his toga like a cape. D-Day looped up his motorcycle chain and wore it around his neck. Stork's toga was inscribed with formulae and geometric diagrams, Hardbar's with pinball art. Bluto had simply stepped through a sheet and tied the corners in crude knots at each shoulder; he looked like a huge, dirty baby. The beer was flowin' an' the jukebox blowin' a fuse.

Otis Day pulled Boon aside. "Hey, we ready to play, man. We need some do-it fluid." Boon, an old hand in these matters, had the gin bottle ready. Otis smiled in gratitude and disappeared briefly with the Knights into the furnace room. When they returned, their eyes were bright and they immediately kicked into a smoking version of "Last Night." A great cheer went up and the floor filled with dancing couples.

Upstairs, more dates were arriving. Otter had decided to go dateless tonight, to hover instead,

Richthofen-like, at the edges of the action, occasionally diving in for the kill; at present he was acting as official greeter at the door. Politely, he took each girl's coat, and when she'd gone, dropped it on the floor. The house was filling up. Couples were now dancing in the living room and on the stairs. The floor shook and the walls throbbed with the music.

Flounder pulled proudly up to the house in the Lincoln and hopped around to let Sissy out. He'd just picked her up at the train station, wearing his best suit and a tie. Sissy had on a pretty pink party dress and a string of pearls; she was sixteen, in the eleventh grade at Harrisburg High, and looked very sweet. They pushed through the front door into the house.

Flounder stopped short. What was this? Everyone was wearing *sheets*. D-Day ran by, waving a cup of purple stuff. Flounder caught his arm. "Brother D-Day, what's going on?"

"To-ga to-ga to-ga!" D-Day explained.

Otter stepped up genially to take Sissy's coat.

"Otter! This is Sissy, my girl. This is the guy I was telling you about, Sis."

"Hi," said Sissy, dimpling prettily.

He gave her the otter smile. "You're even prettier than Kent said you were. And what a great dress!"

Flounder was very pleased. "Hey, why don't you two talk while I get us some punch?"

"Good idea," said Otter. Kent hurried off and Otter slipped an arm around Sissy. "Kent's really a lucky guy. Why don't we sit down somewhere?" Gunning his Messerschmitt, he pushed the stick forward and dove.

* * *

Halfway across campus, at Alumni Hall, the Senior Honors Banquet was underway. At the head table were Dean and Mrs. Wormer, Mayor and Mrs. DePasto, Doug Neidermeyer (who, with a color guard drawn from the Pershing Rifles, had earlier brought in the flag), Mandy Peppridge, and, to receive his award as Outstanding Senior of the Class of '63, Gregg Marmalard. The dean was speaking.

"And so I give you an all-American mayor of an all-American town, my friend... Carmine DePasto."

The mayor rose, smiling, and accepted the polite applause of the banquet with the small upward gestures of his hands that always reminded Dean Wormer of the Pope. "Thank you, dean," the mayor began, in his thick Sicilian accent. "It's a great pleasure to be here with you again as we gather to honor those outstanding seniors who make

Faber the fine institution it is, and the town of Faber the great and proud host of..."

Marion Wormer reeled slightly in her seat. "When the hell do we eat, Vernon?" she whispered loudly.

"Be quiet, Marion," the dean whispered back.

"That wop could talk all night. It's nine-goddamn-thirty, Vernon, and I haven't even seen a frigging breadstick."

People were beginning to look; Dean Wormer felt himself turning red. "You're drunk, Marion," he whispered angrily. "Go home."

"Well, thank God for small favors." She struggled to her feet, upsetting her water glass. Mayor DePasto broke off in mid-sentence to see what was the matter.

"Keep talking, Carmine," Marion called to him. "Great speech!" She headed unsteadily for the door.

* * *

The toga party was at an incredible pitch. Three kegs had kicked and the Purple Jesus punch was getting low. The band was playing *all* Boon's favorites and everyone was madly doing the slop, the bop, and, especially, the mashed potatoes. Long lines stood before both bathrooms; new urinary records were doubtless being set.

Pinto stood at the bar, on his ninth Purple Jesus. Where was Clorette? It was definitely getting late and he was beginning to wonder if he'd been shot down. And then, there she was on the stairs, looking around for him. Pinto's heart thudded; she looked adorable. He waved, catching her eye, and gestured her over to the bar.

She rushed up and took his hand. They exchanged smiling, nervous looks. Pinto couldn't think of anything to say right off so he handed her a cup of punch. To his amazement, she threw back her head and drained the stuff in one long swallow.

"I had to wait 'til my folks went out," she explained. "Let's get more punch. It looks like I have some catching up to do." She grabbed the delighted Pinto by the arm and pulled him toward the Purple Jesus bowl.

Boon had taken up a position slightly to the left of the band on their first downbeat and hadn't left since except during breaks, when he attended them in the furnace room, taking hits of do-it fluid and talking about old records. When they returned to their places, so did Boon. He held a beer bottle as if it were a microphone, singing all the words to all the songs along with Otis. Mercifully, he wasn't audible. He was trying not to think of Katy. Which wasn't too hard, standing up here with the Knights where he could see Hoover and Hardbar and D-Day dancing it up with some of the Delta girls, and Stork doing his peculiar variation of the "mess around" with Flamingo, and Bluto working out with JJ, another Delta girl, doing his strange, hunched, Quasimodo step... well, he meant, this was *it*, man. Prime fun! This was what *life* was about. He whooped into his beer bottle and did a split like Jackie Wilson.

* * *

Into the Delta front yard screeched a Buick; it smashed into the wreck of the old yellow Crosley and stopped. Marion Wormer climbed out. Taking a belt from her flask, she weaved up the walk into Delta House. The noise and energy and stink of sweat almost knocked her back out the door, but she held on and Otter came rushing over.

"Mrs. Wormer!" He offered his arm. "So glad you could come."

"Cut the crap and get me a drink."

Otter offered Marion his arm and took her upstairs to his room. He went to his ambience control center and touched a switch. The ceiling light came on. He dimmed it to a more intimate level with a rheostat and pressed another switch. His sound system activated, emitting Stan Getz softly. Marion smiled. Otter touched a third, switch. The bar lit up, creating twinkling highlights on the many bottles. Marion's smile widened. Otter flicked a final switch and warm lighting caressed the simulated leopard skin of his bedchamber. Marion laughed in delight.

Otter took her coat, carefully put it on a hanger, and dropped it on the floor. He stepped behind the bar, tossed ice cubes in a pair of glasses, and filled them with Johnny Walker Black. Marion was wearing a strapless evening gown that accented her cleavage. She really *wasn't* bad. There was a tie around Otter's neck that he was wearing with his toga; he loosened it now, like Sinatra.

Marion's eyes never left Otter as she took the glass he offered her and drained it. Otter set the empty glasses on the bar, went up behind Marion, and slowly unzipped her dress. She stepped out of it, revealing a good body nicely packaged in black underwear. He put the dress carefully on a hanger and dropped it on the floor. Then he picked her up and carried her to the bed.

* * *

Pinto and Clorette were twisting together, very close, exchanging heated soul kisses during the dips. She had thrown down several more glasses of punch and by now was all over him. Pinto was beside himself with pleasure; being with a girl like Clorette was a long-held fantasy now coming true. He hardly dared form the thought - maybe tonight would finally be... the big night. The band went into a slow number and his groin ached for her as she pressed against him.

"Um... would you like to see some of the rest of the house?"

She ran her lips along his neck, up to his ear "Mmmmm-hmmmm."

"ON THE BRINK"

The order of things gets lost. Bluto was walking down to the basement during one of the band breaks and came upon a folk singer sitting on the stairs. How such a person had ever been let into Delta House in the first place was a mystery to Bluto. The guy had a dippy little moustache and hair parted down the middle; he was strumming a Martin guitar. As a few girls in togas listened dreamily, he sang, in clear, high tones:

I gave my love a cherry
It had no stone.
I gave my love a chicken
It had no bone.
I told my love a story...

Bluto grimaced. He ripped the guitar from the singer's hands and smashed it against the wall, once, twice, three times. Guitar shrapnel flew; people ducked and protected their faces with their arms. Bluto handed the splintered remnants of the instrument back to the dazed geekoid. "Sorry, man," he murmured, and continued on his way to the keg.

D-Day, with a great rebel yell, skied naked down the stairs into the front hall. He slammed into a bunch of dancers and lay on top of them, laughing insanely.

At midnight, Otis Day and the Knights played a forty-seven-minute version of the Isley Brothers' "Shout." It was the single greatest rendition of "Shout" ever heard in Delta house, or perhaps in the world. A considerable number of people passed out during it and had to be tossed onto sofas.

The Purple Jesus punch was long gone. Boon tapped the ninth half-keg of the night.

Bluto found a large jar of mustard. "Bright!" he thought. "Yellow!" He took a chair in the living room, opened the jar, and peered inside. The stuff heaved around in there when he moved his hand, a disgusting yellow sea. "Nice!" thought Bluto. Holding the jar in front of his eyes, he tilted it and watched the pretty mustard flow onto his chest. When the jar was empty, he began to rub it all over himself, trying to cover as much of his body as possible. "I'm the mustard man," he sang. "I'm the goddamn mustard man."

Mountain reeled up to Maida, one of the Delta girls, and lifted toga before her eyes. "You know what this is?" he roared.

Maida stared quizzically. "It looks like a penis, Mountain. Only smaller."

Boon found Otter standing by the painting of the Faber Mongol on the wall near the bar. He waved his hand in the

direction of the shrieking and the dancing. "It always surprises me to see people act this way," he said, very drunk.

"Nothing human offends me," stated Otter.

"Where's your date?"

Otter shrugged. "Let's go see."

They made their way upstairs and stood with Hoover under the moosehead. Marion Wormer, on the shoulders of Hardbar, Dumptruck, Mumbles, and Roach, was being carried in great drunken circles, round and round the living room. She was wearing only one of Otter's sheets, laughing hysterically.

Bluto roared into the room. *"I'm the goddamned mustard man!"* He plowed into Dumptruck and everyone fell

in a huge heap of sheets, flesh and beer. As Marion sat up shakily, D-Day stepped up to her. Kissing her on each cheek, he placed around her neck a toilet seat painted with a laurel wreath.

Hoover shook Otter's hand. "Congratulations. Your date just won the Miss Congeniality Award."

"Thank you. Hoov," said Otter humbly. "It's a great honor."

* * *

Hoover woke Pinto and Clorette around three. She was still very drunk and couldn't really walk. Hoover helped get her into the shopping cart on the front porch, and Pinto set out to wheel her home. Her mumbled directions were a little hard to follow but, once on the right block, it wasn't hard to pick out her house; every light in the place was on. Pinto pushed the cart up the walk.

Near the front porch, an iron lawn jockey held a sign: HON. CARMINE DEPASTO - MAYOR.

Holy shit, thought Pinto wildly. He pushed the cart up to the door and took off like a shot.

"Won' you lemme take you on a sea cruise," sang Clorette.

The door opened; Mayor DePasto stepped out, pulling his bathrobe together. He saw his daughter and his eyes went wide. Blocks away, Pinto could still hear his screaming in Italian.

* * *

"*My* fault? For Chrissakes, Carmine, how the hell could it be my fault?" Dean Wormer sat on his bed, holding the phone. Beside him, laughing drunkenly, was Marion, wearing the same filthy, torn sheet she'd come home in.

"Some goddamned fraternity, I suppose," he said into the phone. Marion was putting her feet in his face. He hated it when Marion put her feet in his face. "No, but I've got a pretty good idea." He struggled to continue the conversation, despite the feet. "I'm gonna string 'em up by the balls, that's what!"

Marion laughed harder, curling into a helpless ball, and fell off the bed.

THE DAILY

"News is Knowledge"

Vol. 16, No. 25

MONDAY, OCTOBER 29, 1962

DELTA PROBATION
Local Teenager Molested

Homecoming Parade Set for Nov. 3

By Hugh Jardon

Members of the Panhellenic Council will sit in judgment of Delta Tau Chi fraternity today at ten o'clock on a number of student deportment violations stemming from an all-night "toga party" held over the weekend.

"It was unbelievable," stated prosecution witness Carl Green, president of neighboring ZTB fraternity. "At first we thought someone was slaughtering livestock in there. The screaming and the breaking things went on until six-thirty in the morning, which is when they began fire-bombing our parking lot. They completely creamed my Valiant."

Other witnesses alleged that passing co-eds were literally dragged into Delta House by a "squat, animal-like figure wearing a bed sheet and smelling of beer and vomit." The kidnapper, as yet unidentified, fits the description of a man seen prowling Sorority Row in recent weeks dressed like a criminal.

A young woman, Faberian fact-ferreters found, was seen entering Delta House in a blue crinoline formal and leaving in a Food King shopping cart. She was reportedly yelling, "I'm the mustard girl! I'm the goddamn mustard girl!" For denied knowl-

ported over one hundred phone complaints from residents as far away as three miles from the fraternity house. "Most of them called about the terrible noise," said Mayor Carmine DePasto, "but three, one of them my sister, got billiard balls through their windows or roofs. Nobody puts a billiard ball through my sister's roof. Some punks are going to pay big. Don't print that."

Dean Wormer told this reporter, "The worst I can do to them is revoke their charter and call in the sanitation department. The actual building was condemned three years ago, but no wrecking crew will risk getting near it."

Other interesting methods of demonstrating the pleonasm, or redundant sentence, is to simply say nothing over and over again. This may be done by repeating empty syntax or patterning the fruitless exercise along an aesthetic direction that leads only to circular, solipsistic verbal statements which contain literally nothing but their own self-referential, quantitative reality. The illusion of qualitative content may, of course, be demonstrated by the elaboration of an idea that is not actually present, like here.

Other interesting methods of demonstrating the pleonasm, or redundant sentence, is to say nothing over and over

The streets of Faber will be served November 3 for College's annual Bathroom Bowl Parade. All eligible fraternities and sororities are to submit float designs to the office by the end of the week.

"Entries will be judged on the basis of topicality and clever jokes like last year," said Dean Wormer.

Last year, it will be remembered, the Delta fraternity entry consisted of a paper figure of Dean Wormer bending over, with a sign captioned, "I like to kiss myself and I'd like to kiss myself..."

"While I admire the ingenuity of making fun of my position," Dean Wormer said, removing his cigar shortly before the spectator's laughter, I find the originality...

— continued on page

Trial

BERIAN

MORE PEP WEEK BEGINS TODAY!   10 CENTS

HEARING

rs. Wormer to Vacation in Saratoga Springs

Mrs. Marion Wormer will be enjoying "a much-needed rest" in Saratoga Springs, New York, a one-page press release from Dean Wormer's office reports. The mimeographed handout says the attractive First Lady of the Campus has been looking forward to the resort's fine horse racing for some time.

"This is not just some spur-of-the-moment thing to get me out of town," Mrs. Wormer said carefully over the phone after it rang twenty-seven times. "Far from it. Nothing to hide here, kid." Then Dean Wormer got on the extension and this reporter suddenly lost my connection. I called right back, but they must have gone out because it rang two hundred and seven times.

All of us at Faber wish Mrs. Wormer a wonderful vacation, and hope the Daily Faberian will soon be able to find out exactly where in Saratoga Springs she can be reached should the key witness to a bizarre hit-and-run spree regain consciousness.

"It was a terrible thing," Mrs. Wormer stated over the phone. "I hope they find him. The driver, I mean. I'm sure it was a man that stole my wagon and hurt that poor person after creaming all those mailboxes. My lawyer says those are Federal offenses. That car-stealer certainly is in a lot of

hot water. This terrible tragedy is a bad shame."

Mrs. Wormer last made the Faberian front page this past spring when she presented the May Queen with the traditional dozen long-stemmed roses while singing a song of her own composition about what she wouldn't give for a chance to display her own talents as a person who receives attention at football games. Hello? Look, for what this reporter is being paid for this, you're fucking lucky I don't tell you about my childhood—the midnight attacks of intestinal flu while Mom and Dad were in their room with the door locked and I know they could hear me ask for just a glass of ginger ale. I'll never forgive you both for that. I hope you get the flu and then see how you are. I wanted it with a Flav-Vor straw. And with some ice.

I want to stop writing now.

Missile Stalls Lunchline

the Daily Faberian

...sence of Russian Com-
...missiles recently discov-
...uba has brought about a
...plans for a joint Commun-
...erican space program and
... line traffic in Faber's Mon-
...Cafeteria.
...Nobody wants the Sloppy
...ex," a highly placed food ser-
...ces official stated today. "The
...ds are eating out, spending their
...y on pizza and illegal beer
...the meal tickets are

Vietnam War Almost Over

Professor Samuel Nerdlanger told sophomores today in Poli Sci 101 that "the conflict in Indochina has just about run its course. The ...are bushed and run-

"but look how well Californians have put up with Hawaii, for example."

Last year Professor Nerdlanger was awarded a $15,000 grant from the Henry Cabot Lodge ...ciation for Eastern Studies ...Nerd."

An extraordinary session of the Panhellenic Council Disciplinary Committee Student Court was scheduled for ten o'clock Monday morning at the Faber Law School's mock courtroom. Gregg Marmalard arrived early, feeling smug and ready to lower the boom. As president of Panhellenic, he would chair today's proceedings. Quite a few students were already milling around the room; it looked as if word of Delta's disgraceful exhibition over the weekend had gotten around. Gregg took his seat in the center of the raised judges' bench and conferred briefly with Doug Neidermeyer, who would be acting as prosecutor. Then Babs Jansen stepped over to him.

"I'll bet it was Eric Stratton," she told him confidentially.

Gregg was interested. "You know that for sure?"

"No, but you'd be surprised at some of the girls he's had." She paused meaningfully. "*Very* surprised."

Worry lines creased Gregg's forehead. "I'm sure I would."

Boon arrived at the courtroom building shortly before ten. Students were streaming in the doors, talking animatedly; he was reminded of people he'd seen in movies, attending public hangings.

Katy walked up to him. "Must've been quite a party."

"Unbelievable. A new low." Boon wasn't quite sure how to react to Katy at the moment. Was he mad at her or was she mad at him? Or was neither of them mad? It was getting all confused. But he wasn't feeling comfortable. That he knew.

"Gee, I'm almost sorry I missed it," Katy said. "What'd you do? Live animal sacrifice? Female circumcision?"

Boon laughed. "No, just a little harmless fun. Hey, buy me dinner tonight?"

A gavel was pounding inside. Katy began to move toward the door. "Can't. Busy tonight."

"Busy tonight?" Boon muttered, frowning. He let Katy pull away from him and disappear in the crowd. What did "busy" mean? But he had no time to think about it; Otter and Hoover were waiting for him. He trotted to the rear entrance of the building and went inside.

At the judges' bench, Gregg was gaveling for order. The courtroom was packed now. The crowd broke into two segments as it flowed into the room. The pro-Omega segment seated behind Doug and Chip at the prosecutor's table, and the Deltas with their friends and hangers-on behind the defendants' table, as yet unoccupied. The pro-Delta contingent was wearing absurd jacket-and-tie combinations that made a mockery of the rules for proper courtroom dress. Well, let them; the Deltas would be getting theirs today.

Dean Wormer came in the rear door. "Let's get the hell going," he told Gregg.

Gregg gaveled. "Please take your seats."

Otter, Boon, and Hoover filed in, wearing suits and carrying briefcases. The Delta section cheered. Hoover uneasily tried to shush them. Boon and Otter held up their briefcases and pointed at them proudly. Otter's briefcase was actually his black doctor's bag, and several Delta girls made loud wolf whistles. Hoover rolled his eyes. Otter and

Boon waved greetings to Gregg and Dean Wormer, and sat down.

"This meeting of the Panhellenic Disciplinary Committee will now come to order," said Gregg. "We'll waive minutes and proceed directly with the charges against Delta Tau Chi. Mr. Neidermeyer?"

Doug stood up. "The following charges are brought: first, that Delta House did knowingly violate the rules governing pledge recruitment by serving alcoholic beverages to freshmen, and after established drinking hours."

Hoover cleared his throat. "I'd like to answer the charges one at a time, if I may."

Dean Wormer, pacing restlessly behind the judges' bench, speared a finger at Hoover. "You'll get your chance, smart guy!" To Doug, he said, "Get on with it."

In the gallery, the Deltas exchanged looks. It looked like a royal ream job coming up, as expected.

Doug consulted his notes. "Secondly, that for the fifth consecutive semester, Delta has achieved a deficient aggregate grade point average."

Hoover tried again. "Half the houses on campus last year didn't make grades, so..."

At a nudge from Dean Wormer, Gregg gaveled loudly, cutting Hoover off. "You'll speak when you're *told* to speak and not before," the dean said sharply. He turned to Doug. "Read."

The Deltas rumbled in the gallery. Doug rattled his papers. "Third, that the Delta House routinely provided dangerous narcotic diet pills to its members during..."

"That's not true!" cried Hoover.

"Not another word!" bellowed Dean Wormer.

The Deltas rumbled louder; several dissenting fart noises issued from their section. Doug continued, unfazed. "...during midterm examination week. *And*, most recently, that a 'Roman toga party' was held, from which we received over two dozen reports of individual acts of perversion so profound and disgusting that decorum prohibits listing them before a mixed audience."

Several Deltas looked proudly at Bluto. Bluto contemplated his nails modestly.

"These are the charges as recorded 28 October 1962. Faithfully submitted, Douglas C. Neidermeyer, sergeant-at-arms."

"Mumble-buzz mumble-buzz," went the crowd.

Gregg gaveled. "Robert Hoover will speak for Delta House."

Hoover stood up. "I don't think you can judge a fraternity without looking at the many positive qualities of the people in it. I..."

"Mr. Chairman, I think we've heard enough," said the dean.

"But I was told I'd have a chance to..."

Gregg pounded with the gavel. "That's enough!" The noise level in the room was rising. "The court will now render a decision."

Hoover was furious. "Look! You said I could speak! What's the..."

Doug leapt up, snarling. "He said that's it! Are you deaf?"

The dean took Gregg by the arm. "Let's finish this damn thing!"

Crude noises and strange, muffled coughs sounded from the Deltas. "Blow job! Blow job!" they coughed.

"Blow job?" mouthed Dean Wormer incredulously.

"I don't think it's fair!" Hoover protested.

"I'll tell you what's fair and what's not!" shouted the dean.

"Eat me! Eat me!" coughed the Deltas. "Horseshit!"

"Boon," Hoover whispered, "will you tell those assholes to shut up?"

"Hey! Shut up, you assholes!" yelled Boon.

Hoover gulped. Otter laughed. In the rear of the courtroom, Katy shook her head sadly.

Doug's face was very red and a vein stood out on his neck. "Mr. Chairman, do we have to listen to any more of this?"

Otter stood up quickly. "Point of parliamentary procedure!" His ploy took the room by surprise; the crowd settled down a little.

"Don't screw around," Hoover warned. "I think they're really serious this time."

"Take it easy, man," Otter whispered. "I'm in prelaw."

"I thought you were pre-med," said Boon.

"What's the difference?" Otter turned his attention to the gallery and began striding back and forth before the judges' bench. "Ladies and gentlemen. I'll be brief. The issue here is not whether we broke a few rules or took a few liberties with our female party guests." Otter looked right at Dean Wormer and winked. "We did."

The dean's jaw fell. The gallery began buzzing again.

Otter raised his voice. "But you can't hold an entire fraternity responsible for the acts of a few sick, perverted individuals. If you do, then shouldn't we blame the whole fraternity system? And if the whole fraternity system is guilty, then isn't this an indictment of our educational institutions in general?"

The gallery was growing noisier. Gregg gaveled futilely.

"I put it to you, Gregg - isn't this an indictment of our whole American society?" The courtroom was total bedlam. Dean Wormer glared at Otter, trembling with rage. Otter topped the clamor with his righteousness. "Well, you can do what you want to us, but we're not going to sit here and listen to you bad-mouth the United States of America!"

He slammed his bag shut and strode indignantly for the exit. On cue, Hoover and Boon slammed shut *their* briefcases and followed him. The Deltas in the gallery stood and began to file from the room, humming "America the Beautiful."

"You're not walking out on *this* one, mister!" roared the dean. "You're finished! No more Delta! You just bought it, brother! I'm calling your national office! There'll be no more beer! No more parties! No more music! No female visitors! I'm revoking your charter!"

The last of the Deltas went through the door. The dean screamed after them. "No more *fraternity!* You hear me? One more thing and you're all out of this college! You got that? *No more fun of any kind.*"

* * *

A day passed, and then another, while they waited for the ax to fall. Nothing happened. At the keg Wednesday night, Hardbar even suggested that maybe nothing *would* happen, that, through Otter's brilliant oratory, they'd somehow escaped the chopping block. But Hardbar was noted for his lack of realism and no one felt encouraged.

The ax fell on Thursday. Boon and Pinto were returning from lunch at Monsanto Cafeteria. Doug Neidermeyer and some other Omegas were hanging out in their fraternity front yard, watching the gorgeous fall leaves drop from their four stately oaks.

"How's it feel to be an independent, Schoenstein?" Doug called. The Omegas with him smiled and nudged one another.

"How's it feel to be an asshole, Neidermeyer?" muttered Boon.

"What'd he say?" asked Doug.

Pinto and Boon continued along the Row. "This really bites it," said Boon gloomily.

"Hoover says they're not even going to let us enter a float in the Homecoming Parade."

"Some stupid zombies get to ride down the street on a pile of Kleenex. Rah rah."

"Boon, look!"

"Oh, Jesus."

A huge moving van sat in the Delta front yard. A double row of campus cops lined the front walk and number of men from Buildings and Grounds were methodically emptying Delta of its kegs and cases of liquor. Mr. Michelostomy was up on the balcony, prying loose the Delta Tau Chi letters with a crowbar. Hoover, Bluto, Stork, D-Day, Hardbar, and a few other Deltas were watching helplessly.

"Hey, what's going on?" Boon asked them.

"They're confiscating everything!" cried Hoover. "Even stuff we didn't steal!"

Two movers emerged from the front door with one of the pinball games. Hardbar whimpered.

Bluto, simmering with frustration, abruptly turned and began kicking the wreck of the yellow Crosley. "God damn... fucking son of a... bitch bastard... piss-eating cunt-face cocksucker!" He smashed the hood down with his fist and spun to face Boon and Pinto. "They took the bar! The whole fucking bar!"

All at once a Buildings and Grounds man slid on a beer can and fell down the Delta front steps, utterly destroying a case of Jack Daniels. Bluto roared like a wounded mammoth and launched himself at the line of cops. Hoover, Boon, Pinto, D-Day, and Hardbar struggled to hold him back.

Otter pulled into the front yard in his Corvette. Sizing up the situation quickly, he leapt out and slipped a quart of scotch from a case being loaded onto the truck. "Hey, Blu'!" He tossed it to him. Bluto stopped struggling and caught it deftly. Then, before the astonished eyes of Deltas, moving men, and campus cops alike, he threw his head back and poured the entire bottle down his throat. It couldn't have taken ten seconds. Bluto belched and tossed the empty over his shoulder. "Thanks. I needed that."

The jukebox was now coming out the door. Boon swallowed with difficulty. "Christ, Otter, this is awful."

"What are we gonna do?" asked Pinto.

Otter smiled. "Road trip?"

Road Trip

"You *can't* take the car!" cried Flounder, horrified. "My brother would *kill* me. He wrote the *mileage* down!"

Otter put a dime in the hall phone. "Okay, okay, we'll check it out with your brother. Really Kent, if you won't do it for me or Boon, you should at least do it for Pinto. He's your best... Dorf? Hey, man, this is Otter."

"The time at the tone will be six forty-seven... and fifty seconds," said the phone.

Otter chuckled. "Yeah, I know what you mean. Listen, Dorf, we were talking about roadtripping to Dickinson and Kent thought you might not want us taking your car."

"The time at the tone will he six forty-eight... exactly."

"Oh? Great!" He held his hand over the mouthpiece. "No sweat, Kent. Why don't you help Boon and Pinto?"

Boon and Pinto were coming down the stairs with two cases of beer from D-Day's secret refrigerator that the campus cops had missed. "Just put it in the car," Otter called to them. He took his hand off the mouthpiece. "Thanks, Dorf. I'll tell him." Pause. "I won't tell him *that*, you dog. So long, man. And thanks again." He hung up and threw an arm around Flounder's shoulders. "Let's go. He wants me or Boon to drive."

Boon jumped behind the wheel. Otter took shotgun, and the freshmen climbed in back. The car screeched away from the house through a vast mud puddle, sending dirty water in all directions.

"Oh my God!" keened Flounder. "Boon, be careful! Please!"

"Cold beer," said Boon and Otter simultaneously, holding out their hands. Pinto opened two cans and passed them up, then took one himself. Boon began a search of the radio hands for something good.

Darkness was settling outside the car. Boon drummed one hand energetically on the dashboard in time to the music. A six-pack died, and then another.

"For Christ's sake, Flounder, drink a beer," said Boon. "We're gonna have fun tonight. You know - drinking, laughing, getting laid?"

Flounder made no move to open a beer. He was pouting.

Boon regarded him in the rearview mirror "Flounder, either you drink a beer or I run us into that bridge." He veered the car toward an onrushing concrete bridge abutment.

"I'm drinking! Look, I'm drinking!" Flounder snatched Pinto's beer and began gulping it down. Otter and Pinto cheered and Boon straightened the car out. "Roses Are Red" came on the radio.

"Bobby Vinton??" Boon reached frantically for the dial. "Gah! Mondo repulso!"

Four whiz stops, two hours, and a state line later, they passed the sign that said EMILY DICKINSON COLLEGE FOR WOMEN — FIVE MILES.

Flounder was very excited. "I hope mine has big tits."

"At least as big as yours," said Boon.

Flounder finished a beer and opened another. "I hear Dickinson girls are fast. How should I handle it, Otter? What should I say?"

"Just mention modern art, civil rights, or folk music, and you're in like Flynn."

"Are you *sure* we have dates?" asked Pinto.

"Absolutely. Boon, what's that chick's name again?"

Boon pulled a folded-up *Daily Faberian* from an inner pocket of his sports coat and handed it to Otter. Otter opened it and read aloud: "Fawn Leibowitz. Fawn Leibowitz. And she was from Fort Wayne, Indiana. Got it." He set the paper aside.

"Oh, boy, I hope I score." Flounder rubbed his hands together lustfully. "Oh, boy, oh, boy."

Boon rolled the Lincoln through the main gate of the Dickinson campus around nine-thirty. Pinto and Flounder, ankle deep in empty Budweiser cans, stared around hungrily; girls were everywhere. Almost all of them seemed to have leotards, guitar cases, and long, straight, dark hair. They looked very sexy. Boon pulled up to the main dorm, a large, neo-Colonial building with ivy-covered white walls; Otter jumped out and went inside.

"Can I help you?" the student receptionist asked.

She had *very* long, straight, dark hair, hanging from a leather buckle. She looked like she might start singing "This Land Is My Land" any minute.

"Yes, I'm here to pick up my date. Could you ring Fawn Leibowitz for me, please."

The receptionist went pale. "Fawn Leibowitz?" She gulped. "Please wait a minute." She became busy at the switchboard.

Otter strolled to a bulletin board. "Advanced Pottery Seminar," announced one of the notices. "Existential Dance Forms Workshop," said another.

"Shelly? This is Brunella, at the desk. Could you come down here, please?" Pause. "Now!" Pause. "Because a boy just came in to pick up *Fawn*, that's why." Pause. "Thanks."

"Is she coming down?" Otter asked.

"Her roommate is. Fawn isn't here. She..." The receptionist swallowed. "Please excuse me." She got up and ran from the room.

A girl came down the stairs. She was very good-looking, with deep, sensitive eyes and a fine set of bongos. She went to Otter and gravely offered her hand.

"I'm Shelly Dubinsky, Fawn's roommate."

Otter smiled and shook her hand. "I'm Frank Lymon. From Amherst. Fawn's fiancé."

Shelly's mouth dropped open. "Her...?"

"Well, we're engaged to be engaged. Say, what's the matter with everyone around here?"

"Let's sit down, Frank." She led him to a sofa. "I don't know any other way to tell you this, so I'll just tell you. Fawn's dead."

Otter burst into laughter. "Dead? Did she put you up to this? That minx. What a lively sense of humor!"

Shelly handed him a copy of the *Dickinson Voice.*

Otter read it out loud. "Sophomore dies in kiln explosion...?" The paper slipped from his hands. "Oh my God!"

Shelly touched his knee. "I'm terribly, terribly sorry, Frank."

Otter looked glazed. "I just spoke to her a week ago. She was going to make a pot for me." He buried his face in his hands.

Shelly, misty-eyed, put an arm around him. "If there's anything I can do ...."

He took out a handkerchief and blew his nose.

"You're very nice. I really shouldn't impose on you."

"No, please. Anything."

"I don't think I should be alone tonight." He looked at her with great vulnerability. "Would you... go... out with me?"

Shelly smiled and stood up. "I'll get my coat."

When she'd almost reached the stairs, Otter called to her, "And could you get three dates for my friends?"

Shelly introduced the girls to Boon, Pinto and Flounder. Boon grabbed Beth, the best-looking of the three, and helped her into the front seat. Otter and Shelly also squeezed into the front seat, and Pinto and Flounder climbed into the back with the other two girls. Otter started the car and they pulled away.

They drove aimlessly along winding, wooded roads. Pinto sat with Brunella, the girl from the reception desk, and Flounder was with the worst-looking of the girls, a tall, grim-visaged individual with extremely thick glasses that made her eyeballs look huge. Her name was Noreen; she hugged the door desperately so that no part of her body touched Flounder's.

The front seat was so crowded that Beth had to crawl onto Boon's lap. "Could you move your hand, please?" she asked him tightly.

"That's not my hand."

"Thanks a lot, Shelly," Beth said. "I'll remember this."

"Pinto, I think I... need another beer," Otter almost whispered. Shelly looked at him, biting her lip. Pinto handed Buds around.

"Pinto? That's a funny nickname," said Brunella. "Why do they call you that?"

"Uh... I'm a quarter Cherokee."

Flounder smiled at Noreen. "Modern art, civil rights, and folk music are my big interests. How about you?"

"Nah, those things really bore me." She wrinkled her nose. "What smells like bacon fat in here?"

"There's a hootenanny at the coffee house tonight," Shelly said brightly.

"Oh, that sounds like fun," said Boon.

"And all the proceeds go to SNCC," said Beth.

"Snick!" said Boon. "Hey, great."

Several more beers were demolished.

"Are we just going to drive around and *drink* all night?" said Noreen. "I'm getting carsick."

"Frank?" said Shelly. "Can't we stop somewhere?"

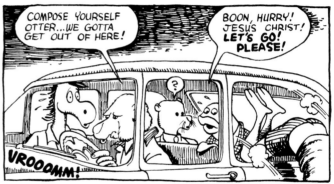

Shelly, Brunella, Beth, and Noreen walked briskly along Route 33, headed back to Dickinson.

"What baffles me is why Fawn would have gone out with boys like that," said Beth angrily.

"They reminded me of *criminals*," whispered Brunella.

"They were horrible!" declared Noreen.

"Oh, I don't know," Shelly smiled. "I thought Frank was quite a hunk."

"*Eeyew!!*" squealed the others disgustedly.

The Lincoln tore along the Pennsylvania Turnpike. Its front and rear ends were mashed horribly and there were great dents in its sides. The tail pipe, unmoored, dragged behind, sending up a sheet of sparks like the wake of a speedboat. Pinto and Flounder were asleep in the back seat. Otter and Boon sipped maintenance beers in front, conversing quietly. Boon's mind, no matter how hard he struggled to control it, kept hurling pictures of Katy at him. Tonight's "date" – his first with someone other than Katy in over a year – had reminded him how grim it was, meeting new girls. He'd had zip to say to her. Boon firmly believed that most people were assholes. It followed that most girls were assholes. What was it Hardbar had said one night at the bar? There were only "pockets of sanity" out there among all the assholes in the world, and the Delta House was one of them. Well, Katy was another. She was, unquestionably, not an asshole. In fact, she was the hottest shit woman he'd ever met; he realized that now. How could he have let things slide so far with her? It would be a crazy thing to do, but he felt like calling her right now, in the middle of the night.

"Boon. Check out Flounder."

Boon glanced in back. Flounder was sleeping with his head against the window; a strand of drool dangled from his open mouth. Otter chuckled and worked the automatic window control. Flounder's window slid open and his head lolled out, abruptly exposed to a seventy-five mph wind.

Flounder woke with a start. "Where are we? How come we're not home yet?" He twisted nervously, looking out all the windows, trying to get some fix on their location. "Otter, don't do this to me! Where're we *going*?"

Boon was punching holes in the top of an empty Bud can. "We're going to California."

Flounder squealed with dismay. "Nooooooo! Please!"

"Jesus, he even wakes up whining," said Otter.

Pinto sat up, rubbing his eyes. He had a headache and felt grumpy. "What? What's going on?"

"Larry, please, tell 'em to stop! We *can't* go to California."

"We can do anything we want," said Otter, exhilarated. "We're college students!"

Pinto leaned over the front seat. "What time is it? Are we really going to California?"

Boon levered down the top of his empty beer can and began pissing in it. "You'll enjoy this a whole lot better if you stay very, very drunk." He slid his window down and tossed the full can into the night.

Pinto and Flounder dutifully opened fresh Budweisers. Soon both boys' spirits had lifted. Boon decided he would call Katy as soon as they stopped somewhere. In the meantime, he led the group through several rousing R&B oldies, singing both the bass and the falsetto parts himself. They had all reached that state of glassy-eyed, drunken plateau that feels almost like sobriety, but isn't. Any of them could have drunk an infinite number of additional beers; the road trip, theoretically, could last forever. And with all the unpleasant shit waiting for them back at school, it wouldn't be bad if it did.

Around dawn they found a twenty-four-hour diner and got some takeout hamburgers. Boon went to the pay phone by the bathrooms. When he returned to the car, he looked grim.

"What'd Katy say?" Otter asked through a mouthful of burger.

"She wasn't home! Where could she be at five-thirty on a Friday morning?"

"What's with you two?"

Boon frowned. "I don't know. Something's wrong."

"Women!" snorted Flounder ruefully. "Can't live with 'em, can't live without 'em."

Otter and Boon looked at Flounder in amazement.

When they finished eating, they regretfully began the trip back to Faber. A gradual depression settled over the car.

Black Friday

Friday, November 5, was a terrific day for most of the students at Faber. It marked the opening of Homecoming Weekend, which meant parties, dates, football excitement, and most of all, the big Saturday morning parade. On Main Street, the mood was festive. Student volunteers were building a grandstand and putting up bunting and banners reading GO FABER MONGOLS and WELCOME ALUMNI. The Pershing Rifles were drilling at the athletic field, practicing the series of maneuvers they would perform in the parade. They were having a wonderful time. But some profoundly awful conjunction of stars must have been hanging over the Delta House, for the day that awaited the brothers would go down as the worst in Delta history.

It was a lousy day for Gregg Marmalard, too. During the afternoon, as he worked on the joint Omega-Tri Pi parade float, Babs Jansen set her long-planned strategy into operation. The float was called "Camelot" and featured a giant, pâpier-maché head of President Kennedy. Gregg was on a ladder, half in and half out of JFK's left nostril.

"Ya'll ready for more pâpier-maché, Gregg?"

"Keep it coming, Babs. This is a bigger job than I thought. I sure hope we finish in time."

"What?"

Gregg extracted himself from the nostril. "I said I hope we finish. Do you know where Mandy is? She was supposed to come over and make teeth."

"Sure don't, Gregg. She *said* she was just going to wash her hair."

"That's typical. Just when we're doing something important." He began to re-enter JFK's nose.

Babs sensed that the moment had come. She burst into tears. "Oh, Gregg, I hate to see her making such a chump out of you."

Gregg pulled his head back out, shocked. "What are you saying?"

"I'm saying that Mandy and Eric Stratton are having an affair!" She wept as Gregg, looking stricken, flapped his mouth wordlessly. "But / love you, Gregg," she declared. "That's why I had to tell you."

Inwardly, Gregg reeled with anger and dismay. He struggled to keep it from his face. "I'm *glad* you told me. The truth sometimes hurts, but the truth *is* the truth."

"That's true," sniffled Babs.

"And I know someone who's going to be hurting a lot worse." He pounded his fist into his palm, smiling grimly. "Babs, I want you to do me a little favor."

* * *

Bluto was hanging out with D-Day in the Delta garage when he spotted the wreck of Flounder's brother's Lincoln pulling into the driveway. He rushed to meet it, then walked along beside it, thumping on the hood with his fists as it lurched into the garage and wheezed to a stop. D-Day's eyes got very wide and he came to his feet, staring in amazement at the once-proud Lincoln as its left front door fell off.

"Hey hey!" said Bluto, excited. "How'd it go, you guys? Who got laid? Who got laid?"

Pinto stepped out of the car. He looked gray.

"Hey, Pinto!" Bluto threw an arm around his shoulders. "Get any? Hah? Little hose job? Hah? Hah?"

Pinto smiled wanly. "I gotta get some sleep." He walked out of the garage with his hands thrust in his pockets, yawning hugely.

Boon climbed out. Bluto punched him playfully in the arm. "Boon, you crazy guy! Get one off? Hah? Hum job? Flying clam?"

"I'm out of here." Boon headed for the door.

"Where you going?" Bluto loved road trip stories; why was everyone leaving?

Flounder climbed from the car and turned to look at it. A groan turned into a whine in his throat and he began to cry.

Bluto was utterly dismayed. What kind of road trip had this been? He decided to cheer Flounder up. "Hey!" he said. "Lookame, lookame." He made several of his best faces.

Flounder scarcely glanced at him; tears were streaming down his face.

Bluto picked up an empty Miller can. "Flounder!" Flounder looked up. Bluto flattened the can against his forehead. Flounder looked away and cried harder. Bluto

pack. "My advice to you is to start drinking heavily."

"Better listen to him, Flounder," said D-Day. "He's pre-med."

Flounder finally got it, the Delta secret: all of life was beer! Sighing, he peeled a can off and began to drink.

"There you go!" said D-Day enthusiastically. "Now, just leave everything to us." He lowered his face mask and touched the flame from his acetylene torch to the Lincoln's right fender.

* * *

Dean Wormer stuck his head out of his office. "Did you get the grade reports on the Deltas yet?"

"Oh," said Miss Leonard, flustered. "Yes, I have them right here."

The dean snatched the folder from her excitedly. "Why didn't you tell me?" He opened the folder and skimmed through the reports. A smile broke over his face. "Oh, good," he crooned. "Oh, good good good."

Mountain opened the Delta back door. "Otter! On the horn!"

Otter trotted out of the garage and went to the phone. To his surprise, the voice on the other end belonged to Babs Jansen, with a most surprising message.

"Are you sure, Babs? Why would Mandy wants to see me?"

"Well, I don't know, Otter. You'd have to ask her."

found an empty Jack Daniels bottle. "Kent!" Flounder looked again. Bluto smashed the bottle over his head and smiled hopefully. Flounder was inconsolable.

Otter climbed from the car, stretching luxuriously. Kent looked at him and started crying harder.

D-Day slid from under the car and came to his feet, rubbing his hands briskly. "Hey, stop blubbering. When I get through with this you won't even recognize it."

Otter took a beer from Bluto and put his arm around the miserable freshman. "Come on, Flounder! You can't spend your whole life worrying about your mistakes. You fucked up. You trusted us. Make the best of it. Maybe we can help you."

"It's easy for you, isn't it?" Flounder snuffled. "What am I going to say to my brother?"

Otter rubbed his chin. "Tell you what. I'll call Dorf I'll swear you were doing a great job taking care of his car... but you parked it out front last night and this morning it was gone. D-Day takes care of the wreck, we report it to the police, and Dorf's insurance company buys him a new car."

Flounder looked briefly hopeful. "Will it work?"

"It's got to work better than the truth."

"But what if it *doesn't* work? What if we got caught? We could get in serious trouble! What if they send an *insurance detective* here? He could have *lie detector* equipment! I could never..."

Bluto solemnly handed him a six-

Babs's room was almost totally pink. The walls were pink, the bed-spread and curtains were pink, even the telephone was pink. One hundred pink stuffed animals covered every available surface, and Babs herself was wearing a pink cardigan. Gregg, a small blue island in his Faber letter sweater, sat beside her on the bed, slowly strangling a pink stuffed bunny.

"As soon as you can get there," Babs continued into the phone. "Well, do you know the Rainbow Motel on Old Mill Road? She'll be in room 103."

Babs hung up. Gregg shivered with anticipation. He punched the bunny's felt face, smashing it to the floor.

Otter put the receiver back on the hook, puzzled but not displeased. He checked out his hair in the mirror, skipped out the back door, and jumped into his Corvette.

Flounder emerged from the garage, a gigantic, silly smile on his face. Following Bluto's prescription, he'd killed another six-pack; he was headed into the house to take a whiz. When he pushed through the back door, he found the phone ringing. He reeled over to it and grabbed the receiver.

"It's your dime, douchebag. Start talkin'."

Hoover, curious, walked over to listen.

"Yeah?" said Flounder to the phone. "Well, I never heard of you."

"Who is it?" Hoover asked.

"Some guy named Gene Wormer. He sounds like a..."

Hoover tore the phone away from Flounder. "Hello, this is Robert Hoover. Who am I talking to?"

"This is Dean Wormer." The dean sat behind his desk, the Delta grade reports spread out in front of him. He trembled with excitement. "I want to see you and the fol-

lowing boys in my office immediately: Eric Stratton, Donald Schoenstein, John Blutarski, Daniel Day, Lawrence Kroger, and Kent Dorfman."

"May I ask why, sir?"

"Because I just got your grades!" The dean hung up and clapped his hands with joy.

"What'd Gene have to say?" asked Flounder thickly.

Hoover was holding the dead phone, looking shell-shocked. He slapped Flounder across the head. "Wake up, you jerk! *Dean Wormer* wants to see us in his office right now!"

Flounder absorbed the news. "Uh-oh," he said, grinning drunkenly.

Boon headed for Katy's, dogged by a sense of impending doom. Except for those few moments at the trial, he hadn't seen her since before the toga party. He'd been hoping all along that eventually she'd start to see things his way again and call him. But she hadn't, and now Boon wondered if she wanted to talk to him at all.

He went to the door of her tiny, off-campus house and knocked. There was no answer. Jesus, what if she were sick or something? He pushed the door open and went in.

Katy wasn't sick. She was walking out of the bedroom, wearing a Faber T-shirt and nothing else. She looked terrific. Boon smiled. "Hi, Katy. I missed you."

Katy looked at him in shock. "Boon!"

"Who's out there, Katy?" called a deep, male voice from the bedroom.

Boon stared at her for an agonizing moment. He recognized the voice.

Katy stared back. "I don't know what to say, Boon."

Neither did Boon. He turned and went out the door.

"Boon, wait!"

The bedroom door opened and Dave Jennings walked out. "Is anything the matter?" Katy didn't answer. Jennings shrugged, kissed her on the forehead, and went into the kitchen to feel around the upper shelves of the cabinet for some matches. The back of his sweater lifted, revealing his ass. Katy regarded it sourly, then turned to look again out the door. Boon was gone.

She slapped her forehead. "Shit," she said softly.

* * *

Otter swung the Corvette into the parking lot at the Rainbow and bounded from the car. He carried his black doctor's bag and a big, wrapped bouquet of flowers. He hadn't the slightest idea

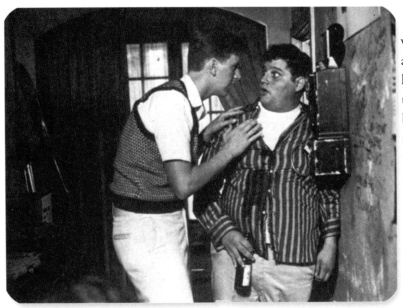

why Mandy had changed her attitude, but it never hurt to be prepared, he reasoned. He knocked at room 103.

The door opened slowly. "It's Mr. Thoughtful," called Otter gaily, "with some beautiful roses for a beautiful..." Stepping inside, he found himself facing Gregg Marmalard, Doug Neidermeyer, Chip Diller, and several other Omegas. He counted them quickly. "One, two, three, four, five... well, looks like we'll be a couple of flowers short. Some of you will just have to share."

Gregg's lips curled into a snarl. He threw a right to Otter's jaw, knocking him back against the door.

Otter rebounded and Doug brought his knee up hard into Otter's stomach, doubling him over. The rest of the Omegas piled on.

* * *

Dean Wormer was in heaven. He leaned back in his desk chair and regarded the five boys lined up before him.

"Where are the other two? Stratton and Schoenstein."

"We looked everywhere," Hoover told him earnestly, "but..."

The dean cut him off with a wave of his hand. "Never mind." He leaned forward, barely able to contain himself. "Have you all seen your midterm grades?"

"Ah... they're not posted yet, sir," said Hoover.

Dean Wormer smiled broadly. "Well, *I've* seen them." He opened a folder on his desk. "Kroger. Two C's, two D's, and an F. That's a one point two grade average. Congratulations, Kroger – you're at the top of your pledge class."

Pinto rocked nervously and looked at the floor. "Dorfman."

"Hello." Flounder was still very drunk. He wavered on his feet like an inflatable rubber toy in a wind.

"Zero point two." He gazed at Flounder with disgust. "Fat, drunk, and stupid is no way to go through life, boy."

Flounder swallowed and his eyes filled with tears. He was beginning to look green.

"Mr. Hoover, president of Delta House. One point six. Four C's and an F. A fine example you set."

For once, Hoover could think of nothing to say.

"Mr. Day. No grades at all. Five courses – five incompletes."

D-Day stared at the Dean with loathing.

Dean Wormer pulled the final grade report from the folder and read it with supreme delight. "Mr. Blutarski. Zero point zero." He looked up triumphantly. Bluto had a pencil hanging from each nostril.

The dean slammed his hand on his desk and stood. "Now, I want you to tell Mr. Stratton and Mr. Schoenstein what I'm about to tell you."

"What's that, sir?" Hoover asked. "You're out! Finished at Faber! Expelled! All of you! I want you off this campus by nine o'clock Monday morning. And tell whoever's still living in your ex-fraternity house to be out of there, too. We're padlocking the place!"

Hoover gulped. "Can you at least tell us why?"

"Why? *Why?* Is it possible that you really don't know? Well, let me fill you in. I'm talking about a dead horse. I'm talking about the daughter of a public official nearly raped at a party. I'm talking about a rotten, criminal element that doesn't have an ounce of respect for our institutions. You're out! All of you! And that goes for your two missing friends, too. I'm calling your parents tomorrow." The dean sat back in his chair, feeling warm chills of pleasure course through his body. "And I'm sure you'll be glad to hear that I've already notified your local draft boards and told them that all of you are now eligible for military service."

Flounder's mouth fell open. He staggered forward, placing both hands on the desk. "Well?" said Dean Wormer.

Flounder's jaw moved up and down but no words came out. *"Well?"*

Flounder's larynx bobbed. He couldn't seem to find his voice.

"Out with it!" snapped the dean.

All at once Flounder's face contorted horribly and his cheeks puffed out. A look of horror came over the dean's features and he made an attempt to fling himself out of the way. Too late. *"Hurrraaaaaaaalp!!"*

That night, Gregg Marmalard took Babs Jansen parking at Pencil Point. He sat next to her, smiling triumphantly. Her hand was busy in his lap.

"Well, Otter certainly had it coming," she said.

"I don't think the Deltas will be giving us any more trouble," he said smugly.

Babs looked down at her hand. "Gregg, is it supposed to be this soft?"

* * *

Sounds of music and merriment could be heard up and down Fraternity Row as the Friday night Homecoming parties got under way. The kegs were flowing and couples kissed beneath the trees. But Delta House was quiet. The brothers were strewn around the living room like the shattered survivors of some terrible war.

Bluto lay flat on his back on the floor. "Christ! Seven years of college down the drain. Might as well join the fucking Peace Corps."

"My mother's gonna kill me," said Pinto miserably.

Hoover had his head in his hands. "I knew it... I knew it... I knew it..."

Flounder sat next to Boon on the sofa beneath the moose head, looking very remorseful. "I can't believe I threw up in front of Dean Wormer."

"Face it, Kent," said Boon. "You threw up *on* Dean Wormer."

"Oh, no," Kent groaned. "What is it with me, Boon? What's my problem? How come I'm not cool?"

"Cool? You're a fucking hero! Nobody ever booted on Dean Wormer before."

"And *you* never booted *at all* before," pointed out Hardbar. "You made great strides today, Kent. Bluto always said you'd..."

"What? Over?" Bluto looked aghast. "Did you say it's over? *Nothing's* over, till we decide it is! Was it over when the Germans bombed Pearl Harbor? Hell, no!"

Otter looked at Boon with a curious smile. "The Germans?"

"Forget it," whispered Boon. "He's rolling."

"And it ain't over now!" Bluto declared. "When the going gets tough..." He paused, waiting for someone to finish the line. No one did, so Bluto finished it himself. "The tough get going! Who's with me? Let's go!" Bluto trotted out of the room as if he were leading a troop assault.

Nobody else moved. There was a brief pause and Bluto walked back in, looking even more determined. "What the fuck happened to the Delta I used to know? Where's the spirit? Where's the guts?" He rushed over to Hardbar and took his dispirited face in both hands. "Hardbar! Hey hey, whaddaya say? Huh?" Hardbar looked glumly back at him, too depressed to answer. Bluto grabbed Stork by the shoulder and shook him. "Stork, you madman! Are you with me?" Stork couldn't even meet his eyes.

"Mothball!" Bluto spotted the skinny freshman sitting on the arm of one of the sofas. Wrapping an arm around his neck, he lifted him into the air. "Up, big fella!

The front door slammed open and D-Day appeared, supporting Otter, whose face looked like it had been stuck in a hamburger machine. The brothers watched in horror as D-Day helped him to a sofa.

"Jesus Christ!" cried Boon. "What happened? You're grotesque!"

Otter spoke painfully through battered lips. "Some of the Omegas did a little dance on my face."

Bluto was seething. "Who was it?"

"Oh, Greggie and Dougie and some of the other Hitler youth."

Boon shook his head. "Why? What did you do?"

Otter thought it over. "I don't know. They're just animals, I guess." He looked around the room at the depressed, disconsolate faces. "I get the feeling I missed something here."

"Yeah, you did," said Boon. "We're all officially kicked out of school. Wormer got our grades."

"Kicked out of school," Otter repeated slowly. "That makes sense."

"Hey!" Bluto was standing up, his hands on his hips. "What's this lying around shit?" he asked the room. "We just gonna take this?"

"What the hail we *spoze* to do, ya moron?" asked Stork.

"War's over, man," said D-Day quietly. "Wormer dropped the big one."

Let's go go go! Everyone – follow me!" He trotted again from the room, carrying Mothball with him.

The Deltas stirred listlessly, but no one joined him. Bluto walked back in. "You pussies." He dropped Mothball on the floor and regarded the brothers with contempt. "This could be the greatest night of our lives and you're gonna let it be the worst." He made his voice high and tremulous, mocking them. "Oh, we're afraid to go with you, Bluto. We could get in trouble."

"Well, you can just kiss my ass from now on!" he roared. "Not me! I'm not taking this! Wormer? He's a dead man. Marmalard? Dead! Neidermeyer...?"

"Dead!" Otter painfully stood up. "Bluto's right. Psychotic, but absolutely right. *We've got to take these bastards.*"

Now that Otter was talking, the Deltas began to pay attention. Gradually their eyes cleared and they sat up. Maybe something *could* be done.

Otter limped to the center of the room. "Now we could fight them with conventional weapons, but that could take years and cost millions of lives. No, in this case, I think we have to go all out. This situation absolutely requires a really futile, stupid gesture on somebody's part."

Bluto swelled his chest proudly. "And we're just the guys to do it!"

The Deltas were excited now, stirring and talking to one another.

"Let's do it!" said Boon.

"Yeah!" Bluto raised his fist in the air and bellowed, "Let's do it!"

The brothers leapt to their feet, cheering, and rushed from the room; except Pinto, who remained seated, a half smile on his face.

"Hey, Lar," called Flounder excitedly. "You comin' with?"

"I'll meet you guys later. I've got something else to do first."

* * *

It was midnight when Pinto reached the DePasto house. He took a guess regarding the location of Clorette's room and tossed a pebble at the window. No response. He tried again. Still nothing. He chose a larger pebble and threw it. The window shattered loudly.

Pinto almost fled, but a light winked on behind the broken window and suddenly Clorette was there, rubbing her eyes, peering into the night. She was wearing the cutest nightgown Pinto had ever seen. He felt a tightness at the back of his throat.

"Tommy?" she called softly.

Pinto's face fell. "Tommy?" he said to himself. He clicked his flashlight on and beamed it onto his hopeful, upturned face. Clorette, evidently recognizing him, smiled and waved, then disappeared from the window. A moment later the front door opened and she came out.

"Hi," whispered Pinto. He clicked the light on and off and Clorette joined him under the tree.

"Hi."

"I'm Larry. Remember me? I took you to a party."

"I was *there,* remember? Wait for me a minute, while I get dressed. Okay?" She darted back to the darkened house. Pinto beamed.

Five minutes later they stood together on the sidewalk. "So how come you show up now?" Clorette asked him. "I didn't expect to *see you.*"

Pinto considered and rejected the idea of telling her that he wouldn't *be* in Faber any more, after the weekend. "Well, I never got to say goodnight after the party."

"No kidding. They almost pumped my stomach."

Pinto shifted his feet nervously. "Listen, would you like to go for a walk or something?"

"What do you mean, 'or something?'"

"Well, I could get some beer...."

Clorette took his arm. "Not this time, okay? You might get lucky without it." She smiled up at him, and Pinto felt his heart begin to pound.

They stopped at his dorm; Pinto ran in and grabbed Kent's sleeping bag. Then they went to the athletic field where Pinto had done his ROTC drilling, spread the bag out on the fifty yard line, and climbed inside. They made out for a long time, an item or two of clothing coming off every few minutes. Pretty soon, Pinto was down to his shorts. He was uncomfortably aware that, on top of all the other firsts that were going on here, Clorette was about to become the first girl ever to see his spotted dong. He'd been dreading this moment for years; probably it would be best to get it over with. He told Clorette the story of the tar, then held the bag open and shone the light inside so she could see for herself.

"That's why they call me Pinto," he told her with intense nervousness.

Clorette looked at him and smiled. "You know something, Larry? You're a very interesting person."

Pinto felt his heart soar. *She hadn't pointed to it in horror and screamed, "Mutant!"* He pulled Clorette to him and kissed her with feeling. Then he had another thought.

"Before we go any further, there's something else I want to tell you. I lied to you. I've never done this before."

Clorette regarded him curiously. "Never made out with a girl?"

"No," said Pinto quickly. "I've never done what I think we're gonna do in a minute. I *almost* did once, but..."

Clorette kissed him. "That's okay, Larry. Me neither."

Pinto kissed her back, then reached inside the bag to help her off with her panties.

"Besides," Clorette said, "I lied to you, too."

"Oh, yeah? What about?"

She dropped the panties out of the sleeping bag. "I'm only thirteen."

* * *

Back at the Delta garage, the air was full of sparks from D-Day's torch, and the sounds of drills and hacksaws almost drowned out the cries of revelry from the rest of the Row.

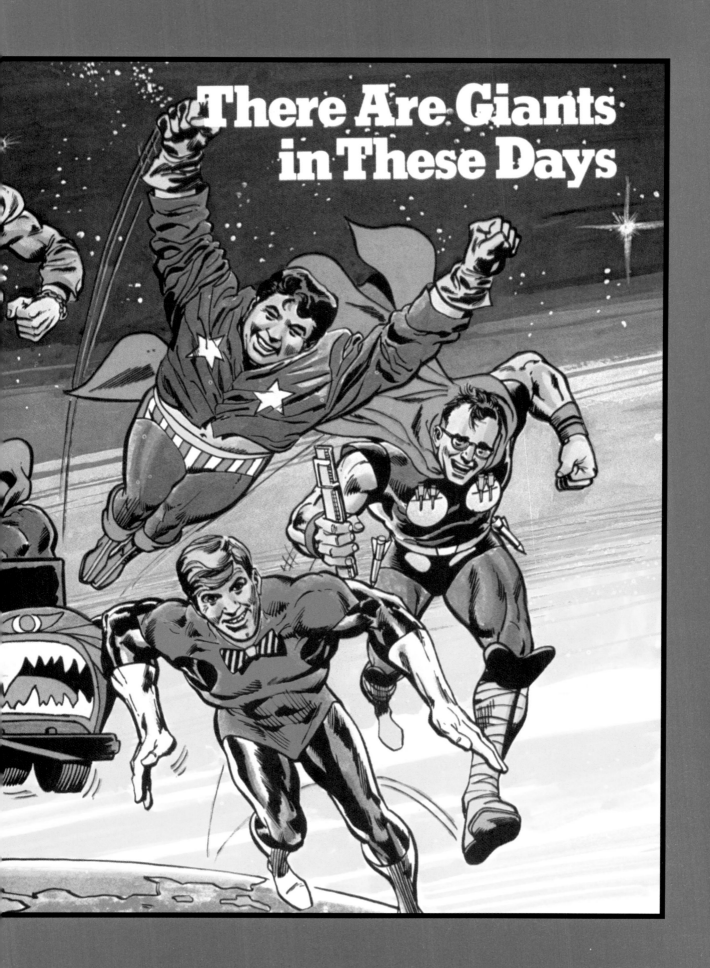

The day dawned clear and crisp; football weather, the perfect Homecoming Saturday. A cheerful excitement suffused the campus. Members of the Faber marching band, resplendent in their uniforms, began to leave their dorms, toting trumpets, tubas, and glockenspiels. On the Row, frantic last-minute finishing touches were being administered to floats.

There was a single hint of things to come, and in the good-natured hustle and bustle of parade preparations, hardly anyone noticed it: the head of the statue of Emil Faber was gone, cut off cleanly at the neck.

By ten-thirty, the last bunting had been draped on the reviewing stand and the final sawhorse barrier placed along the curb of the parade route. Mr. Michelostomy was testing the microphone of the VIP box. Main Street gradually became crowded, as townspeople, visiting parents and alumni, Faber students, and swarms of excited kids mingled cheerily beneath the canopy of colorful GO FABER MONGOLS banners.

At ten forty-five, Faber police, assisted by student marshals, began to move the crowd behind the barriers. Hoover arrived. He wore a black raincoat and extremely dark shades, and clutched a heavy satchel. "Excuse me. Oh, I'm sorry." He made his way through the crowd. "Pardon me. Official business. Sorry." A couple of kids were sitting on the mailbox in front of the Book Nook. "Okay, you kids, off the mailbox – that's government property. Let's go! Move!" The kids climbed down hastily and ran away through the crowd. Hoover stowed his satchel beneath the mailbox and sat on it himself.

A block and a half down, Stork and Hardbar, also in raincoats and dark glasses, shouldered their way through the crowd and took up positions at curbside. They stood unmoving, grimly purposeful. A man tapped Hardbar on the shoulder.

"Excuse me, but could you let my kids stand in front of you? They can't see."

"No," said Hardbar.

At ten fifty-five, an Oldsmobile convertible carrying Dean Wormer, Marion Wormer, Mayor DePasto, and Mrs. DePasto moved slowly up the parade route. The dean and the DePastos waved cheerily to the crowd, drawing a smattering of applause. Marion sat motionless, hung over and scowling.

"Smile, Marion. Please," whisperd the dean.

"I may vomit."

Katy, at the curb, absently snapped pictures for the parade coverage in the *Daily Faberian*. Where was Boon?

She had to talk to him, let him know she'd broken it off with Jennings, that she was deeply sorry about yesterday. She'd figured she'd run into him for sure today, but so far she hadn't seen him. In fact, she hadn't seen any of the Deltas yet. She looked around anxiously and spotted Hoover perched on a mailbox. She threaded her way through the crowd to him.

"Hey, Hoover, have you seen Boon?"

Hoover pretended not to hear her. He was wearing dark glasses and peering around sneakily, like some sort of Balkan spy. She slapped him impatiently on the leg.

"Ow!"

"Hoover, where's Boon?"

He looked at her reluctantly. "Ah... Katy, I don't think you should stay around here."

She blinked. "What are you talking about?"

"We all got expelled yesterday."

"What?" Katy was shocked. "Why? Where's Boon?"

"Katy, listen to me. I think you'd be glad later if you weren't here now." Hoover returned to his scrutiny of the street and refused to say another word. Katy moved off through the crowd, totally confused.

If she'd happened to glance into the Faber Five and Dime, the mystery would have deepened. Flounder was inside. "May I have ten thousand marbles, please?" he was asking the startled salesgirl.

*   *   *

The Oldsmobile, one of the best from Mayor DePasto's dealership, stopped before the reviewing stand. The bleacher seats were filled with college officials and alumni bigwigs; they applauded politely as the dean, the mayor, and their wives sat down in the VIP box. Gregg Marmalard, awaiting them there in a suit and tie, shook hands all around.

The mayor went to the microphone. "It gives me great pleasure to present this ceremonial goldplated whistle to 1962's honorary grand marshal, Dean Vernon Wormer. Mr. Marshal, the streets of Faber are yours."

The dean took the whistle from the genially smiling mayor. Creating an even bigger, more genial smile on *his* face, he held the whistle up for the photographers and blew it with an exaggerated puffing motion.

As the whistle sounded, there was a great flourish of snare drums from the Faber marching band. The parade emerged from its staging area and began moving slowly up Main Street. The crowd cheered, waving Faber Mongol pennants and blue and yellow pompons. Children jumped up and down. Small dogs cavorted excitedly.

Two red Oldsmobile convertibles headed the procession, bearing the Homecoming Queen and her court of five princesses. The girls wore pink, frilly dresses, jeweled diadems, and pearl necklaces; each carried a bouquet of roses. They waved and smiled to the crowds. Next came the Faber marching band, playing a spirited "Stars and Stripes Forever," and then a dwarf elephant and his trainer, wearing a long black cape. To the delight of the children, the elephant began waving its trunk at the spectators.

On the mailbox, Hoover checked his watch – eleven o'clock.

In an alley, standing by his bulging gunnysack of marbles, Flounder checked his watch – eleven o'clock.

Seated behind a steering wheel in the Delta front yard, D-Day checked his watch – eleven o'clock.

Nearby, in a dark, enclosed space, Bluto lit a match and checked his watch – five-thirty.

"Let's move out," said Otter, slapping D-Day on the top of his helmet.

"Yah-hah!" cheered Boon.

The peacefulness of a deserted Fraternity Row was broken by the roar of powerful engines. From the Delta front yard slowly pulled a late, unscheduled parade float. It was a crudely-rendered birthday cake with eight teetering candles; on its side was the simple message, EAT ME. The cake turned in the direction of the parade and, with a great screeching of tires, roared forward.

The gaiety on Main Street was unbounded. The Omega-Tri Pi Camelot float was now driving slowly up the block to warm applause from the crowds. The giant Kennedy head had been finished in time and looked great. It was topped with an arc of letters reading the new frontier. In front of the swaying JFK head stood four Jackie Kennedys, wearing identical pink A-line suits, pillbox hats, and white gloves. Mandy and Babs were the two foremost Jackies they smiled prettily and waved to the crowds.

The next float belonged to Zeta Tau Beta, the Jewish house. It portrayed a giant white hand shaking a giant black

hand beneath a banner reading ALL MEN ARE BROTHERS. The crowd applauded politely, then cheered as a group of girls in cowboy hats and short shorts rode by on horses. A clown gamboled along behind them with a trick dog leash that seemed to hold an invisible dog. The children shrieked with glee.

The float of the fun-loving GEKE house followed, an enormous Playboy rabbit in a Faber letter sweater, surrounded by busty co-eds in bunny costumes. The rabbit's head was hooked up to a small motor so that it swiveled foolishly back and forth. On the float's side was the inscription, WHEN BETTER WOMEN ARE MADE, FABER MEN WILL MAKE THEM. The men in the crowd chuckled and nudged one another.

The playful rabbit float was followed directly by the highly serious Pershing Rifles in their dress berets, shoulder braid, and gleaming, spit-shined boots. Doug Neidermeyer, tall and proud, marched at their head, calling cadence. Their M-1s swirled and flashed in the sun as they performed their maneuvers with flawless, machine-like precision. The crowd, greatly impressed, applauded enthusiastically.

Dean Wormer nodded to the mayor. "Fine parade. Very orderly."

"Wonderful," said Mayor DePasto. "Just wonderful."

Marion yawned, wishing for her flask.

Stork and Hardbar, stony-faced, checked their watches. They exchanged a nod and Stork moved off through the crowd.

Hoover checked his watch, climbed off the mailbox, and retrieved his satchel. "Pardon me. Excuse me. Sorry, coming through. Excuse me."

The birthday cake zoomed along the deserted campus streets, ignoring all stop signs.

Babs smiled and waved to the crowd. "Now, Mandy honey, I hope we can still be friends."

"I hope you die," said Mandy, smiling and waving.

"Well, sugar, if that's your attitude, maybe you better give me Gregg's pin right now."

"I don't have it."

"I suppose I'll just have to get it myself, then."

"You better change first. I flushed it down the toilet."

Stork emerged from the crowd at curbside. The Faber marching band approached; the bandleader twirled his fancy baton in dazzling circles, then tossed it, still spinning, high in the air. Stork lurched up to him, stiff-legged,

head bobbing, and hip-blocked him perfectly, sending him flying into the crowd. Stork neatly caught the descending baton and suddenly was leading the band, who, intent on their music sheets, never noticed the transfer. He twirled the baton once or twice and made an abrupt left face into an alley. The band played on, following him obediently.

The birthday cake reached the edge of town. It ran a red light and veered down a side street.

Stork's preselected alley ended in a brick wall. He waited until the last moment, then ducked aside.

The jaunty Sousa air gave way to mad honks, smashings, and cries of dismay. Nearby spectators looked at each other curiously.

Hoover reached his objective – the telephone pole on the corner by the Book Nook. Opening the satchel, he pulled out a heavy chain ending in a large, vicious-looking hook. He affixed the hook to the telephone pole, then ran backward into the street, playing the chain out of the satchel as he went. When he reached the GEKE float, he hooked the other end of the chain to its rear bumper, admired his handiwork briefly, and disappeared back into the crowd.

The chain stretched taut. With a loud crack, the telephone pole snapped at the bottom and fell down into the street. The crowd screamed, rushing frantically to get out of the way. The bunny float was torn to bits; its front end was flung sideways, into the curb. Spectators scrambled for safety as the co-ed bunnies catapulted into the air.

The birthday cake rounded a corner and sighted the tail end of the parade – a second marching band and the traditional Faber Mongol float with its giant Mongol head. On its side was the inscription, CENTRAL NORTHEAST WESTERN DIVISION CONFERENCE CHAMPS. Two senior lettermen, wearing Genghis Khan costumes and carrying footballs, stood at the front of the float, waving wooden swords at the crowd. One of them noticed a giant birthday cake headed towards them.

"Say, those guys are moving pretty fast," he said to the other Mongol. They raised their swords and waved them at the cake, gesturing for it to slow down.

The cake accelerated. It tore through the marching band, which scattered, screaming, and slammed into the Mongol float, driving it off the street into a fire hydrant. Spectators hurled themselves out of the way; the two football-carrying Mongols flew from the front of the float. The hydrant snapped and water shot up to spray from the giant Mongol's nose, mouth, and ears. The crowd stirred uncertainly, then broke and ran.

Three blocks up, at the reviewing stand, the smashing and screaming were clearly audible. The dean grabbed Gregg by the tie and jerked him over. "What the fuck is going on down there?" Gregg could only shrug and stammer helplessly.

Chip Diller, in his student marshal's armband, tried to calm the frightened crowd. "Hold your places! There's nothing to worry about! Don't panic!"

The giant Mongol's head blew off. Water geysered high in the air.

* * *

Pinto blinked and woke up. He was lying in Clorette's arms in the sleeping bag. And they were in the end zone! He couldn't believe it, but he'd finally done it. *He was no longer a person who'd never been laid.*

Henceforth, no matter how long he lived or where he went or how bad things got, laid was something he would always have been! Gradually, his euphoria was penetrated by the sounds of screaming and loud crashes. He sat up.

"Oh my God, the Homecoming Parade!" He shook Clorette, kissed her quickly, and then they were stumbling into their clothes, rushing toward Main Street.

* * *

Doug Neidermeyer stared about, wild-eyed. The crowd, screaming and mindless, rushed in all directions around him. "Let's stop this now!" he barked to the Pershing Rifles. "Ten-hut! Port arms! *Charrrrge!*"

The Rifles rushed toward the cake, shouting a battle cry. Flounder suddenly appeared before them at the curb and spilled his gunnysack into the street. Ten thousand small colorful spheres rolled beneath their feet; the Rifles flew into the air and came down hard. "Shit!" they yelled. "Hail! Whut th' fuck?" Each time one of them managed to get to his feet, he'd take one step and fall again.

"Get up, you faggots!" screamed Doug. "Get up and fight!"

Inside the birthday cake, Otter laughed. "Flounder just took out the Rifles. This is beautiful, man!" The arrangement was like the inside of a tank. Otter and Boon shared the turret, calling directions and encouragement to D-Day, who was driving blind. "Hey, D, guess who's next?"

"The Bund boys?"

"You got it."

D-Day whooped and jammed the accelerator to the floor.

The birthday cake rammed the Omega-Tri Pi float. The Jackie Kennedys squealed and held on to their standposts desperately. The float jumped the curb and struck a lamppost. Babs started to topple off. Mandy made a grab for her and caught her by the sleeves of her A-line suit. Babs kept going; the suit stayed where it was. Babs stood up shakily, composing herself, then felt a wind and looked down to find herself wearing only bra and panties. *"Eeeeeeeee!"* she shrilled, and made futile efforts to cover herself with her arms.

"All is well!" Chip Diller shouted at the crowds. "Don't panic! Stay calm!" Nobody paid any attention to him.

In an alleyway near the reviewing stand, Hardbar took a bundle of smoke bombs from his raincoat. Mothball and BB braced the homemade Delta mortar, previously a standing ashtray, and Hardbar dropped the bombs into it. They ducked quickly, like movie mortar teams. *Toomp!* The bombs sailed into the very center of the parade, gushing thick white smoke. Amidst screams of fear and shouted curses, Faber students and elderly alumni collided with fleeing clowns and terrified, crying children.

The cake paused only briefly, then leapt toward the ZTB float, smashing into it broadside. The white and black hands disengaged and streaked off in opposite directions. The white hand struck the curb, bounced high in the air and hurtled through the show window of DePasto Oldsmobile.

A cry of agony tore from the mayor's throat. He sprang at Dean Wormer, caught him by the neck, and began strangling him.

Hardbar, in the alley, dumped his remaining smoke bombs into the mortar. *Toomp!* They landed directly before the reviewing stand, spewing red, green, and blue smoke.

The birthday cake entered the smoke and was lost to sight. "Cut the cake!" said D-Day. Otter and Boon sliced through the ropes that held the float together. The two cake halves went flying backward, stampeding the elephant, who, blasting mighty trumpets, lumbered through the slowly reforming Pershing Rifles, sending them sprawling.

The dean and the mayor had death grips on each other's throats.

"Look!" cried Gregg.

Gradually emerging from the wall of colored smoke was an apparition straight from hell – the Deathmobile! Unquestionably, it was D-Day's masterpiece. The chassis was Dorf's Lincoln, with a cylindrical water tank welded where the roof had been, forming a turret. Savage tiger teeth replaced the grill and fantastical dragon fins rose from the rear fenders. Delta signs covered it.

Abruptly, the fearsome vehicle screeched forward and executed a full 180-degree turn that aimed it directly at the VIP box of the reviewing stand. Alumni and college officials stampeded from the bleachers, screaming. The dean and the mayor seemed paralyzed, staring at the Deathmobile as if hypnotized by a snake.

"Those bastards," breathed Dean Wormer. "Those *bastards.*"

The mayor was livid. "I'll throw them all in jail!"

Marion whooped with delight. "Sure beats hell out of last year's parade!"

The trunk ot the Deathmobile abruptly flew open and Bluto catapulted out, a Neanderthal jack-in-the-box, emitting a piercing battle cry. He was wearing all the sweaters and sweatshirts he owned for padding, and a pirate bandanna on his head for style. Thrust in his necktie cummerbund was a giant wooden sword.

A half dozen campus cops rushed up to grab him. Bluto swan-dived into their midst, tumbling them to the ground. Instantly he was up and running, with the cops in hot pursuit. He made it to the wall of the Faber Five and Dime and, apelike, scrambled up the drainpipe as the frus-

trated cops jumped up and down in fury on the sidewalk below. He reached the roof and drew his sword. "Sanctuary!" he roared. "Sanctuary! Sanctuary!"

Inside the Deathmobile, Otter slapped D-Day on the helmet. "Okay, let's take the cheese."

Laughing maniacally, D-Day stamped on the accelerator.

Mayor DePasto's eyes widened as the Deathmobile roared forward. "They wouldn't dare!"

"Ramming speed!" bellowed D-Day.

"I hate those guys," said Dean Wormer weakly.

With a tremendous crash, the Deathmobile tore into the reviewing stand. Wood splintered; banners shredded; debris flew. Gregg, the dean, the mayor, and their wives shot skyward.

"Stay calm!" screamed Chip Diller, his voice cracking with terror. "Don't panic!"

Flounder grinned happily. "Oh, boy, is this *great!*"

He took a seltzer bottle from his raincoat pocket and began tiptoeing toward Doug Neidermeyer.

Doug was breathing very deeply; bits of foam clung to the corners of his mouth. This time the Deltas had gone too far. He took a live bullet from a pocket of his uniform and loaded it into his M-1. The first Delta he saw...

"Hey, Neidermeyer!" called a horribly familiar, whining voice.

Doug brought the rifle to his shoulder, spun, and fired, all in one motion. Flounder's giant grin abruptly switched to a look of abject terror as the seltzer bottle shattered in his hand. He looked up to find Doug rapidly reloading. Good God, he was going to die!

Out of nowhere, the giant black hand careened by. It scooped up Doug and swept him away, screaming curses. Flounder blinked. Doug was gone! Laughing with a greater joy than he'd ever known, Flounder threw his arms in the air and danced a heady jig of victory.

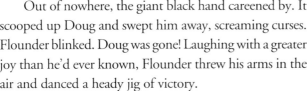

Pinto and Clorette, badly winded, finally reached Main Street. Pinto stared in amazement at the wreckage, smoke, and screaming co-eds. What had he missed?

The mayor stirred feebly in the ruin of the reviewing stand. He blinked; was he hallucinating? His daughter, missing from her bed this morning, was running up to him, hand in hand with a boy in a Delta jacket.

"Daddy! This is Larry Kroger, the boy who molested me last month," Clorette told him excitedly. "We have to get married."

Pinto's eyes widened and he began backing away. "We should discuss this some other time, sir. I know you're very busy right now and…"

"*Rarrrrrr!*" The mayor launched himself at Pinto's throat. Pinto ducked under his closing hands and ran for all he was worth.

Hoover found Dean Wormer sitting motionless on a pile of rubble and squatted down next to him. "Ah… this may seem like an inopportune moment to ask, Dean Wormer, but do you think you could see your way clear to giving us one more chance?"

Gregg Marmalard pulled himself to his feet, shaking his head to clear it. One thought preoccupied him – kill

the Deltas, stomp them, smash them flat. He climbed onto the crumpled Deathmobile and began slamming his fist on the hatch.

"Come out of there, you bastards! You hear me?"

"Who is it?" called a musical falsetto.

"You know damn well who it is!"

"Sorry, you'll have to come back later. We're doing the dishes."

"Goddamn it, get out here! Right now!"

Otter did, but through the trunk. He stood behind Gregg for a moment, enjoying his helpless fury, then tapped him on the shoulder. Gregg whirled around, fists raised. Otter held out his hand.

"Gregg, look at my thumb."

Gregg looked at Otter's thumb. Otter threw a whistling left to Gregg's jaw, feeling the impact down to his toes. Gregg toppled backwards and disappeared into the wreckage of the grandstand.

"Gee, you're dumb," Otter said.

In the crowd, Mandy laughed and threw Otter a thumbs up sign. Otter bowed gallantly, then exited quickly as several campus cops boiled up the side of the Deathmobile toward him.

Boon slipped from the trunk while the cops were straining to open the hatch. As he rushed for the sidewalk, one of them spotted him. Four cops sprinted after him and grabbed him in front of Edith's Cut-Rate. Each grabbed a limb and they began carrying him toward the paddy wagon.

Katy rushed over, a hysterical expression on her face. "Officers, please! For God's sake, they're looting the Food King!"

The police exchanged looks, then dropped Boon and rushed off. Boon climbed to his feet and looked at Katy uncertainly. Screaming townspeople and children rushed by on either side of them.

Katy came into his arms. "I love you, Boon." A wave of happiness and relief broke over Boon. He kissed her and kissed her.

"Stand firm! Hold your places! Don't panic!"

Chip's voice was almost gone, but he still tried gamely to calm the crowds. He heard what sounded like a herd of buffalo charging and spun around. Five hundred crazed spectators, fleeing the black hand, stampeded right over him.

D-Day sidled up to an empty Faber police car. He glanced left and right, then slipped inside. Why, the fools had left their key in the ignition! Throwing his head back, laughing maniacally, he slammed the car into gear and headed for the open road.

Bluto cavorted gleefully on the roof. "No prisoners!" he roared. Abruptly, through the smoke and swirling crowds, he spotted Mandy. A look of sheer happiness came over his face; he dove off the roof, grabbed a "Welcome Alumni" banner, and swung down to the street on it like Tarzan on a vine. He landed at a dead run, swept Mandy into his arms, and, never breaking stride, streaked for the nearest DePasto Oldsmobile. Mandy screamed and tried to break his hold. Bluto dumped her into the back seat of the convertible and jumped behind the wheel. Gunning the engine, he fired out of Faber, toward an uncertain future in the wide, wide world.

The National Lampoon's
Animal House
Book

Where Are They Now?

FABER COLLEGE REUNION COMMITTEE QUESTIONNAIRE
NAME: John Blutarski   **CLASS:** 1963
BIO: Since leaving Faber College after 8 years of study, Mr. Blutarski wed the former Amanda Pepperidge (Faber class of 1963). Relocating to Pittsburgh, PA, Mr. Blutarski rose to the rank of Vice President of U.S. Steel. A desire to serve the public led Mr. Blutarski to seek the office of the United States Senate. Following 3 terms as a Senator, Mr. Blutarski was elected as the 43rd President of the United States, where he continues to serve and lead our nation through these difficult times.

"All the News That's Fit to Print"

VOL.CL .. No. 51,874   NEW YORK, WEDNESDAY, SEPTEMBER 12, 2001   75 CENTS

U.S. ATTACKED
President Blutarski to Mid-East: "See if you can guess what I am now"

"It wasn't over when the Japanese bombed Pearl Harbor, and it's not over now" says White House in revised statement

"Missiles Launched, Problem Solved"
Says United Nations While Applauding President

FABER COLLEGE REUNION COMMITTEE QUESTIONNAIRE

NAME: *Amanada Blutarski*   **CLASS:** *1963*

BIO: *Amanda (Mandy) Blutarski married John Blutarski (Faber 1963) shortly after graduation. A dutiful wife, she supported her husband throughtout his storied career. She now serves as First Lady of the United States, but remains dutiful to her family.*

Her son, John Junior will be enrolling in Faber College this fall.

July 4, 1998

Sen. Blutarski To Run

PITTSBURGH–It hasn't been easy to serve as both a focal point for criticism and a rallying point for his party, but Senator Blutarski has weathered it all with pride. And now, he has a new rea-

announced his cand President of the Unite

"This is a momentou. stated Sen. Blutasrki. "I am here to prove to every American that the pie in the sky is not only reachable, it is edible."

FABER COLLEGE REUNION COMMITTEE QUESTIONNAIRE

NAME: Daniel Shoenstein

CLASS: 1963

BIO: I knocked around New York a bit, driving a cab to make ends meet. I married my Faber sweetheart Katy in '64, but we divorced in '69 (my fault). We met up again in '74 and got married for the second time, but divorced in '85 (her fault). During this time, I tried my hand as a novelist, but didn't have much success.

Katy and I got back together in '94 and married yet again. The divorce is pending (my fault).

For now, I'm heading out to L.A. to meet up with my old Delta Brother Hardbar, who needs some help finishing his "Great American Porn Novel."

Dear Mr. Schoenstein:

Thank you for your submission. I w ...
news, but unfortunately I'm returni ...
use your manscurpt at this time.

Best,

He was a man. More than just being a male he was a man in the classic sense of the word: rugged, chiselled features, thick hands like slabs of smoked Canadian bacon, an impenetrable demeanor as stoic and sold as the proud visages of Mt. Rushmore.

But a male, a man, a man's man...needs a female. In the contemporary climate of talk show psychosis, how could a masculine sort fit in? Every social event listed in the paper mentioned something called Emo – wasn't that the little red guy on Sesame Street? Were singles really so childish? What the hell was wrong with the world?

He needed more than a female. He needed a mature female, a full-blown woman. He followed the model of John Wayne, not that of all the liberal pedophiles running rampant.

The problem was that nobody knew he existed. He went unremembered everywhere he went. Hell, he didn't even know his o ...

Dear Mr. Schoenstein,

... appreciate the humor in DENTAL SURGERY ON A CHICKEN ... f that would not be appreciated by today's modern a ... deed a spoof. If the manuscript you submi ... t you have missed the mark enti ...

of course ...

The X1 chip couldn't be allowed to fall into the wrong hand ...

Roman Jaffe refused to allow it to come to that. With little ... little hope he devised a plan. The fate of everything would depen ...

thing.

A chicken.

Little Pablo next door kept "Ole Roosty" pecking day an ...

FABER COLLEGE REUNION COMMITTEE QUESTIONNAIRE
NAME: Katherine Fuller-Shoenstein **CLASS:** 1963
BIO: I recently retired from the Boston Public School System where I worked as a child psychologist. I have since relocated to Maine where I operate a yoga studio.

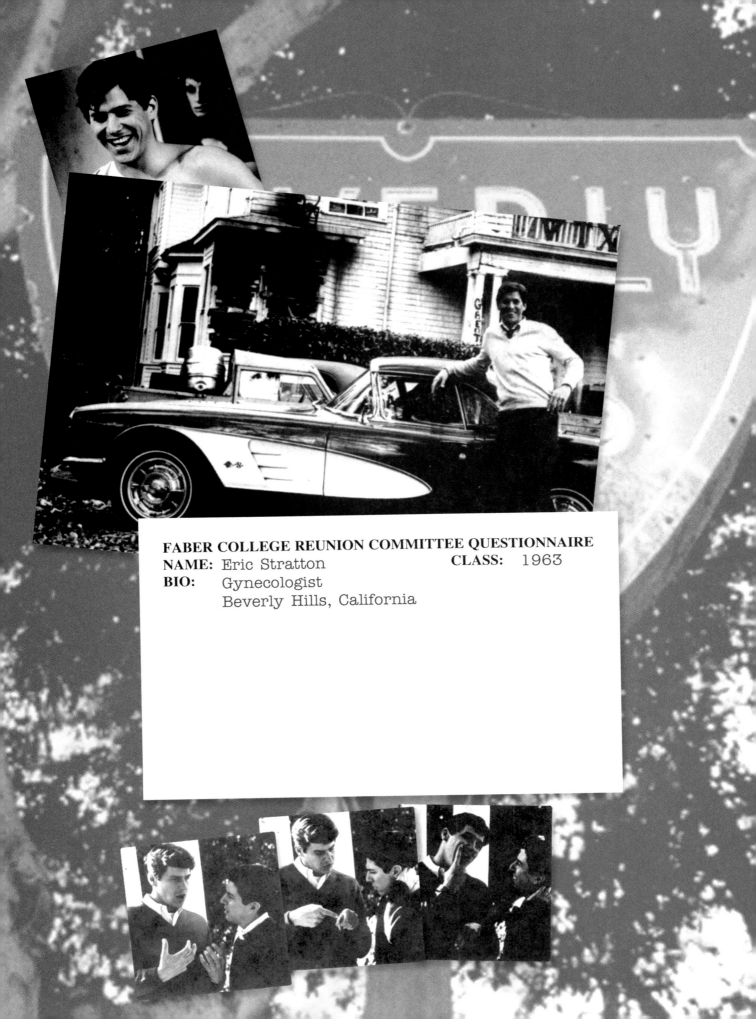

FABER COLLEGE REUNION COMMITTEE QUESTIONNAIRE

NAME: Eric Stratton   CLASS: 1963

BIO: Gynecologist
         Beverly Hills, California

FABER COLLEGE REUNION COMMITTEE QUESTIONNAIRE
NAME: Kent Dorfman   **CLASS:** 1966
BIO: After a long career as a Sensitivity Trainer for the Encounter Groups of Cleveland, Ohio, I founded The Wellness Groups of Cleveland, an organization devoted to encouraging wellness, being well, seeming well, and fortifying one's own wellitude.

    Business is booming since the introduction of my new W.E.L.L.ness Pills (you can find my infomercial on "The Divorce Channel" Sundays, 3:45 a.m.).

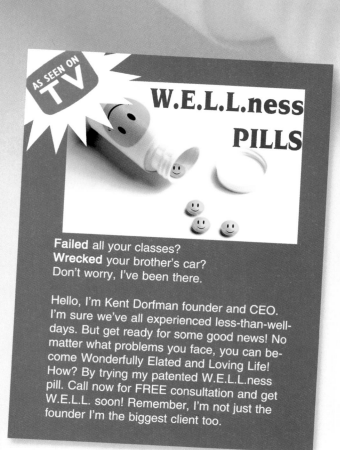

AS SEEN ON **TV**

W.E.L.L.ness PILLS

Failed all your classes?
Wrecked your brother's car?
Don't worry, I've been there.

Hello, I'm Kent Dorfman founder and CEO. I'm sure we've all experienced less-than-well-days. But get ready for some good news! No matter what problems you face, you can become Wonderfully Elated and Loving Life! How? By trying my patented W.E.L.L.ness pill. Call now for FREE consultation and get W.E.L.L. soon! Remember, I'm not just the founder I'm the biggest client too.

UMOR MAGAZINE 75 CENTS

otebook

NATIONAL LAMPOON

Back to College
Scams and Scholastic Ploys • Pages Left out of the Vassar Yearbook
e Adelphian Lodge • Esquire Parody • Famous Student Stunts and Pranks

NATIONAL LAMPOON
The Humor Magazine
$1.00

NATIONAL LAMPOON
DEC. 1974   THE HUMOR MAGAZINE $1.00

IT WAS THEM AGAINST THE RULES...
and the rules lost.

NATIONAL LAMPOON'S
MONSTER
FRAT

MOVIE NEWS

Low Brow Humor Taken to New Heights

Monster Frat rules box office for 8th straight week.

by Josh Newberry

National Lampoon's gross-out comedy is the best coming-of-age film in recent memory. While recent entries to the genre have left movie-goers baffled and disturbed (*Teenagers in Heat*, anyone?) "Frat" has caught the imagination of audiences and critics alike.

The blockbuster has led to a resurgence in college fraternities. Dwindling membership had plagued the organizations for the last decade, but the fil part on the

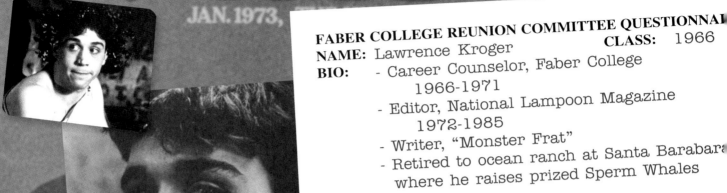

FABER COLLEGE REUNION COMMITTEE QUESTIONNAI

NAME: Lawrence Kroger   CLASS: 1966

BIO: - Career Counselor, Faber College
            1966-1971
        - Editor, National Lampoon Magazine
            1972-1985
        - Writer, "Monster Frat"
        - Retired to ocean ranch at Santa Barabara
            where he raises prized Sperm Whales

FABER COLLEGE REUNION COMMITTEE QUESTIONNAIRE   **CLASS:** 1963
NAME: Robert Hoover
BIO:

- Public Defender, Baltimore Maryland
- Assistant District Attorney, Baltimore Maryland
- Currently teaching English as a Second Language, Los Angeles, California

FABER COLLEGE REUNION COMMITTEE QUESTIONNAIRE
NAME: Daniel Simpson Day   **CLASS:** 1963
BIO:

FABER COLLEGE REUNION COMMITTEE QUESTIONNAIRE
CLASS: 1963
NAME: Gary Dwayne Stark
BIO:
- Holder of several patents
- Founded Stark Technologies
- Status, deceased (choked on a peach pit)

DAILY FABARIAN
Stark Engineering Building Breaks Ground

The ground has broken for the latest addition to the Faber campus, the Stark Engineering Building. Named after wildly successful alumnus and philanthropist Gary Dwayne Stark (Faber, 1963), the engineering school's new building is made entirely possibly by generous funding from Stark Technologies. The building will boast the latest in computer technology, several research and development facilities, a 3,000 square foot gaming room, and a library of books donated by the Science Fiction Writ...

stark technologies

STARK TECHNOLOGIES
Annual Report

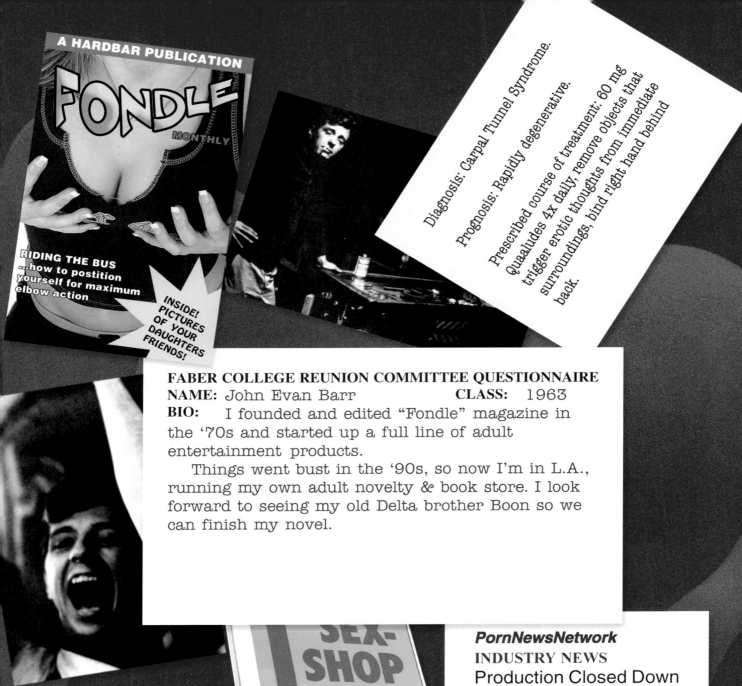

A HARDBAR PUBLICATION

FONDLE
MONTHLY

RIDING THE BUS
...how to postition yourself for maximum elbow action

INSIDE! PICTURES OF YOUR DAUGHTERS FRIENDS!

Diagnosis: Carpal Tunnel Syndrome.

Prognosis: Rapidly degenerative.

Prescribed course of treatment: 60 mg Quaaludes 4x daily, remove objects that trigger erotic thoughts from immediate surroundings, bind right hand behind back.

FABER COLLEGE REUNION COMMITTEE QUESTIONNAIRE
NAME: John Evan Barr   CLASS: 1963
BIO: I founded and edited "Fondle" magazine in the '70s and started up a full line of adult entertainment products.

Things went bust in the '90s, so now I'm in L.A., running my own adult novelty & book store. I look forward to seeing my old Delta brother Boon so we can finish my novel.

SEX-SHOP

PornNewsNetwork
INDUSTRY NEWS
Production Closed Down
Hardbar Video Faces Legal Action Over Claims of Animal Cruelty, Perversion

Local health officials were alerted yesterday to an outbreak of salmonella on the set of *Hook Hand Ho 7*. Preliminary investigations traced the illness to a parrot by the name of "Mr. Munchkin." An unnamed source claimed Mr. Munchkin suffered "godless" acts of animal cruelty on film.

Mayor Nancy Sidelson remarked, "If these allegations prove true, I will personally see to it that Hardbar Video face prosecution."

Hardbar contract girl, Misty Gape, has also been diagnosed with the first known human case of avian syphilis.

PornNewsNetwork
REVIEW
X Marks the G-Spot
Hardbar Video
Format: VHS
Price: $29.95
89 minutes

HARDBAR VIDEO
X Marks the G-Spot

Hardbar Video is pleased to announce the launch of its pirate-themed *X Marks the G-Spot* adult entertainment series. The recent launch of HV, LLC has seen some exciting developments. In addition to the titular release, several other films are forthcoming, including *Thar She Blows, Peg Leg Lesbos,*

HV is confident that consumers in the adult market are longing for something new, and the pirate sub-genre will satisfy even the most jaded customer.

Hardbar Video will debut at the XXO conference in Las Vegas, NV April 23-25. Several cast members will participate in panel discussions and autograph sessions. Vibrating hook hands will be given away a the HV booth.

Hardbar Video began operation with the cult classic *Feelin' Goo Fondle on the Prowl*, a video tie- to the popular men's magazine.

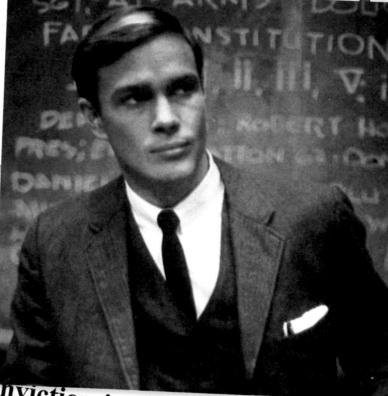

A-2 April 19, 1974

POLITICS

Another Conviction in Watergate Scandal

White House Aide Marmalard Faces 8 Years For Obstruction

WASHINGTON–White House staffer and Nixon aide Gregg Marmalard was convicted for his role in the ongoing Watergate conspiracy. Marmalard, 36, was sentenced to eight years in federal prison.

Weeping openly, Marmalard begged the court for leniency, citing his service to the country, Christian faith, and frat nections.

was G. Gordon Liddy, who described Marmalard as a "first-class twerp" and stated that the Watergate scandal was "all Marmalard's fault" and that Marmalard "single-handedly brought down the greatest president since Lincoln."

When prosecutors inquired into this activity, Marmalard related that, "Mr. Liddy wanted to toughen me up, make a man out of me." Marmalard also to other acti

September 9, 1996

Television

HBO Shoots For Gritty Realism in New Prison Drama

HOLLYWOOD — Known for his memorable portrayals of "bad boy" supporting characters, Stephen Jones has signed on as part of an ensemble TV cast. "This project is big," Jones said. "HBO is starting a prison drama

role is complicated because of the trauma I go through. They brought in an anal rape technical advisor named Marmalard to guide me. He understands the victim's role inside and out. People will remember this per

FABER COLLEGE REUNION COMMITTEE QUESTIONNAIRE
NAME: Douglas C. Neidermeyer   CLASS: 1963
BIO:

- Killed in Vietnam by his own troops.

USARMY
Internal Investigation Of Casualty 11,843 –
Neidermeyer, Douglas
Preliminary Interrogation Records

Specialist Gerdes
Disposition: unreliable. Location at TOD: mess hall. Remarks: "Right about then
I put on Strange Days real loud, and everybody was grooving with Morrison. We
didn't hear shit." Status: AWOL.

Private First Class Arnzen
Disposition: unreliable. Location at TOD: mess hall. Remarks: "We al
Dougie. Too bad we couldn't hear Charlie sneak
tap-dancing stripper giving us a show." Status: AWO

Private LaValley
Disposition: credible. Rema
called 'bean compan
same old f

Distinguished Service to Country Remembered

Douglas C. Neidermeyer, son of Gregor and Samuelina, slain in combat March 15 in South Vietnam's Hung Phatt Province.

An investigation has been launched by the U.S. Army due to the conflicting details surrounding Capt. N

COLLEGE REUNION COMMITTEE QUESTIONNAIRE

NAME: Ronald "Chip" Diller   **CLASS:** 1966

BIO:

- Vice President, DeLorean Motor Company
- Christian Missionary, Senegal
- Investment Banker, Drexel Burnham
- Christian Missionary, Angola
- Assistant CFO, Enron
- Christian Missionary, Mozambique
- U.S. House of Representatives
- Christian Missionary, Federal Correctional Institution, Butner, North Carolina

January 14, 2007

Rep. Diller Nabbed in Kiddie Porn Sting

WASHINGTON—Federal Authorities, working in conjunction with the popular television program "America's Biggest Pervert" nabbed more than the run-of-the-mill online predator yesterday.

Representative Ronald Diller (R-PA) showed up at the site of the undercover sting with a bag of candy, expecting to meet an 11-year-old boy. Instead, he was met by a TV crew and federal marshals.

FABER COLLEGE REUNION COMMITTEE QUESTIONNAIRE
NAME: Hon. Carmine DePasto   1963
BIO: Missing since 1971.
        Rumored to be part of Emil Faber Memorial
Highway.

FABER COLLEGE REUNION COMMITTEE QUESTIONNAIRE
NAME: Clorette DePasto
BIO: Vassar, Class of '70
        Yale Law, Class of '73
        United States Attorney,
        Southern District of New York

FABER COLLEGE REUNION COMMITTEE QUESTIONNAIRE
NAME: Vernon M. Wormer
BIO:

- Suffered massive stroke turing Student
  Demonstrations of 1969.

- Currrently living under 24-hour care in
  Sarasota, Florida

FABER COLLEGE REUNION COMMITTEE QUESTIONNAIRE
NAME: Marion Wormer
BIO:

- Alcoholics Anonymous
  1963-64, 1966-68, 1970 (July),
  1972-75, 1977-1980, 1982-84,
  1985-

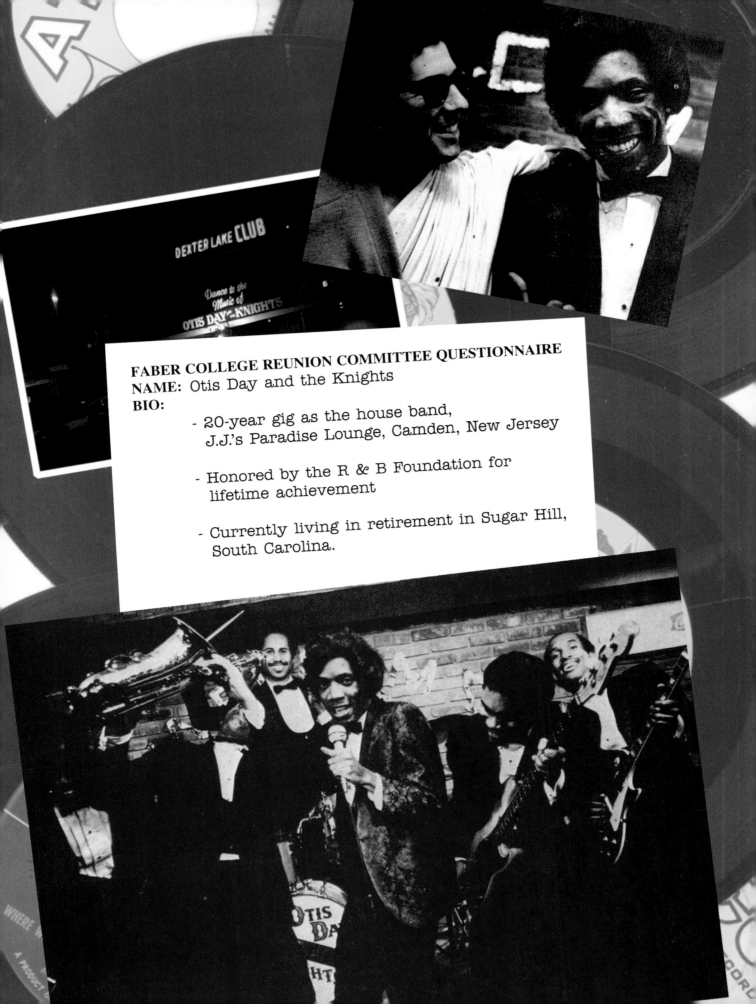

FABER COLLEGE REUNION COMMITTEE QUESTIONNAIRE
NAME: Otis Day and the Knights
BIO:

- 20-year gig as the house band,
  J.J.'s Paradise Lounge, Camden, New Jersey

- Honored by the R & B Foundation for
  lifetime achievement

- Currently living in retirement in Sugar Hill,
  South Carolina.

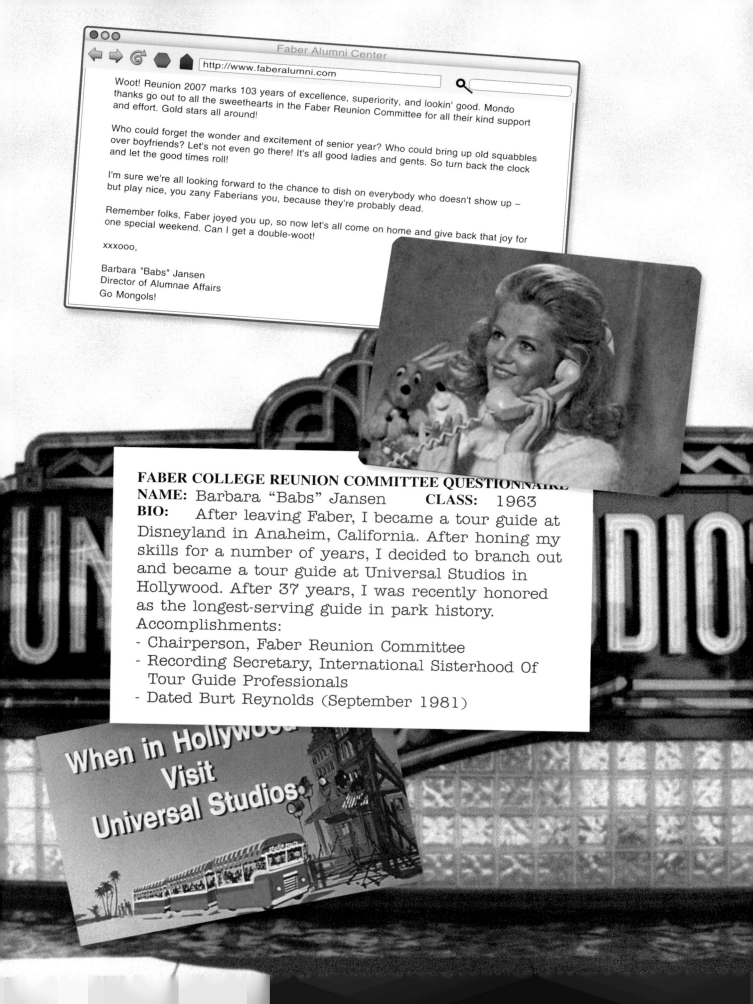

http://www.faberalumni.com

Woot! Reunion 2007 marks 103 years of excellence, superiority, and lookin' good. Mondo thanks go out to all the sweethearts in the Faber Reunion Committee for all their kind support and effort. Gold stars all around!

Who could forget the wonder and excitement of senior year? Who could bring up old squabbles over boyfriends? Let's not even go there! It's all good ladies and gents. So turn back the clock and let the good times roll!

I'm sure we're all looking forward to the chance to dish on everybody who doesn't show up – but play nice, you zany Faberians you, because they're probably dead.

Remember folks, Faber joyed you up, so now let's all come on home and give back that joy for one special weekend. Can I get a double-woot!

xxxooo,

Barbara "Babs" Jansen
Director of Alumnae Affairs
Go Mongols!

FABER COLLEGE REUNION COMMITTEE QUESTIONNAIRE
NAME: Barbara "Babs" Jansen   **CLASS:** 1963
BIO: After leaving Faber, I became a tour guide at Disneyland in Anaheim, California. After honing my skills for a number of years, I decided to branch out and became a tour guide at Universal Studios in Hollywood. After 37 years, I was recently honored as the longest-serving guide in park history.
Accomplishments:
- Chairperson, Faber Reunion Committee
- Recording Secretary, International Sisterhood Of Tour Guide Professionals
- Dated Burt Reynolds (September 1981)

When in Hollywood
Visit
Universal Studios

Last known photograph

Delta Alumni
The Tri-Annual Magazine for our Distinguished Brethren

ARS GRATIA ARTIS

Faber Chapter
Receives Charter

"It took 45 years and and an Executive Order
from President Blutarski, but Delta House
will be reconstituted in time
for the First Son to pledge."

-Gerald Hoffer

President, ΔTX Chapter Affairs

ANIMAL HOUSE BOOK

The Book:

Orientation Booklet &

Daily Faberian .... Douglas Kenney

Copy Editing .... Louise Gikow and Susan Devins

Art Associates .... Ruthanne Hamill, James Cook, and Phyllis Hochberg

Editorial Assistant .... Elise Cagan

Production Manager .... George Agoglia, Jr.

Production Assistant .... Mark Gill

Additional Lettering .... John Workman

Additional Material .... John Lawson and Jay Naughton

With Art By:

Rick Meyerowitz .... Cover

C. Royd Crosthwaite .... Fraternity Row

Wayne McLoughlin .... Rush Week

John Barrett .... Sink Night

Julian Allen .... School Begins

Steve Brodner .... Dean Wormer Remembers

Les Katz .... Pinto's First High

Boris Vallejo .... There Were Giants In Those Days

Mara McAfee .... Bluto's Midnight Peep

Charles Rodrigues .... Mr. Michelostomy

Lou Brooks .... Midterms

Carter Jones .... Toga Party

Shary Flenniken .... Pinto and Clorette on the Brink

Marvin Mattleson .... Road Trip

Warren Sattler .... The Delta Animals at the Road House

Randall Enos .... Black Friday

Dick Giordiano .... There Are Giants in These Days

Mary Wilshire .... Orientation Booklet

Judith Jacklin .... Photo Coloring

John Shannon .... Photography

Christine M. Loss .... Photography

Jay Naughton .... Where Are They Now

The Movie

John Belushi .... John 'Bluto' Blutarsky

Tim Matheson .... Eric 'Otter' Stratton

John Vernon .... Dean Vernon Wormer

Verna Bloom .... Marion Wormer

Tom Hulce .... Larry 'Pinto' Kroger (as Thomas Hulce)

Cesare Danova .... Mayor Carmine DePasto

Peter Riegert .... Donald 'Boon' Schoenstein

Mary Louise Weller .... Mandy Pepperidge

Stephen Furst .... Kent 'Flounder' Dorfman

James Daughton .... Greg Marmalard

Bruce McGill .... Daniel Simpson 'D-Day' Day

Mark Metcalf .... Doug Neidermeyer

DeWayne Jessie .... Otis Day

Karen Allen .... Katy

James Widdoes .... Robert Hoover

Martha Smith .... Barbara 'Babs' Jansen

Sarah Holcomb .... Clorette DePasto

Lisa Baur .... Shelly Dubinsky

Kevin Bacon .... Chip Diller

Donald Sutherland .... Prof. Dave Jennings

Douglas Kenney .... Stork

Chris Miller .... Hardbar (as Christian Miller)

Bruce Bonnheim .... B.B.

Joshua Daniel .... Mothball

Sunny Johnson .... Otter's Co-Ed

Stacy Grooman .... Sissy

Stephen Bishop .... Charming guy with guitar

Eliza Roberts .... Brunella (as Eliza Garrett)

Aseneth Jurgenson .... Beth

Katherine Denning .... Noreen

Raymone Robinson .... Mean dude

Robert Elliott .... Meaner dude

Reginald Farmer .... Meanest dude (as Reginald H. Farmer)

Jebidiah R. Dumas .... Gigantic dude

Priscilla Lauris .... Dean's secretary

Rick Eby .... Omega

John Freeman .... Man on Street

Sean McCartin .... Lucky Boy

Helen Vick .... Sorority Girl

Rick Greenough .... Mongol

Also From National Lampoon Press

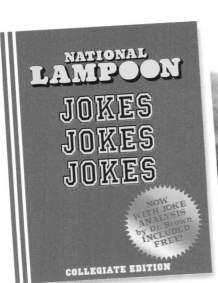

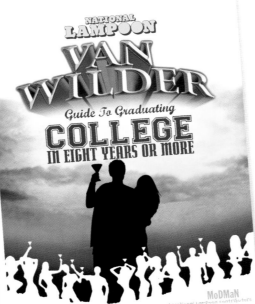

Also by Chris Miller

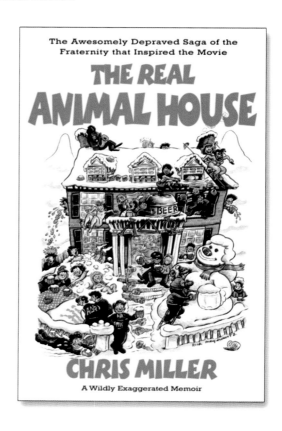